PC Tools™ 7 Quick Reference

Edmund X. deJesus

PC Tools 7 Quick Reference.

Copyright ©1991 by Que Corporation.

All rights reserved. Printed in the United States of America. No part of this book may be used or reproduced in any form or by any means, or stored in a database or retrieval system, without prior written permission of the publisher except in the case of brief quotations embodied in critical articles and reviews. Making copies of any part of this book for any purpose other than your own personal use is a violation of United States copyright laws. For information, address Que Corporation, 11711 North College Avenue, Carmel, IN 46032.

Library of Congress Catalog Number: 90-82439

ISBN 0-88022-829-6

This book is sold *as is*, without warranty of any kind, either express or implied, respecting the contents of this book, including but not limited to implied warranties for the book's quality, performance, merchantability, or fitness for any particular purpose. Neither Que Corporation nor its dealers or distributors shall be liable to the purchaser or any other person or entity with respect to any liability, loss, or damage caused or alleged to be caused directly or indirectly by this book.

94 93 92 91   4 3 2 1

Interpretation of the printing code: the rightmost double-digit number is the year of the book's printing; the rightmost single-digit number is the number of the book's printing. For example, a printing code of 91-1 shows that the first printing of the book occurred in 1991.

This book is based on PC Tools Version 7.0.

Que Quick Reference Series

The *Que Quick Reference Series* is a portable resource of essential microcomputer knowledge. Whether you are a new or experienced user, you can rely on the high-quality information contained in these convenient guides.

Drawing on the experience of many of Que's best-selling authors, the *Que Quick Reference Series* helps you easily access important program information. The *Que Quick Reference Series* includes the following titles:

1-2-3 Release 2.2 Quick Reference
1-2-3 for DOS Release 2.3 Quick Reference
1-2-3 Release 3.1 Quick Reference
Allways Quick Reference
AutoCAD Quick Reference, 2nd Edition
Batch Files and Macros Quick Reference
CorelDRAW! Quick Reference
dBASE IV Quick Reference
Excel for Windows Quick Reference
Fastback Quick Reference
Hard Disk Quick Reference
Harvard Graphics Quick Reference
LapLink Quick Reference
Microsoft Word Quick Reference
Microsoft Word 5 Quick Reference
MS-DOS Quick Reference
MS-DOS 5 Quick Reference
Norton Utilities Quick Reference
PC Tools 7 Quick Reference
Q&A 4 Quick Reference
Quattro Pro Quick Reference
UNIX Programmer's Quick Reference
UNIX Shell Commands Quick Reference
Windows 3 Quick Reference
WordPerfect Quick Reference
WordPerfect 5.1 Quick Reference

Publisher
Lloyd J. Short

Series Director
Karen A. Bluestein

Production Editor
Laura J. Wirthlin

Technical Editor
Lynette Nichols Healey

Production Team
Claudia Bell, Scott Boucher, Sandy Grieshop, Bruce Steed

Trademark Acknowledgments
AT&T is a registered trademark of AT&T. COMPAQ is a registered trademark of COMPAQ Computer Corporation. CompuServe is a registered trademark of CompuServe, Inc. and H&R Block, Inc. dBASE II, dBASE III, dBASE IV, and MultiMate are registered trademarks of Ashton-Tate Corporation. DisplayWrite is a trademark of International Business Machines Corporation. Lotus, 1-2-3, and Symphony are registered trademarks of Lotus Development Corporation. Microrim and R:BASE are registered trademarks of Microrim, Inc. Microsoft Excel, Microsoft Windows Write, Microsoft Word, and Microsoft Works are registered trademarks of Microsoft Corporation. NetWare is a registered trademark and Novell is a trademark of Novell, Inc. Paradox, Quattro, and Quattro Pro are registered trademarks of Borland International, Inc. PC Tools is a trademark of Central Point Software. WordPerfect is a registered trademark of WordPerfect Corporation. WordStar is a registered trademark of WordStar International, Inc. XyWrite is a registered trademark of ZYQUEST, Inc.

Table of Contents

Introduction ix

GENERAL INFORMATION 1
PC Tools Applications 1
Hints for Using This Book 2
Using Keyboard Commands 3
Using the Mouse with PC Tools 5
Using PC Tools on a Network 6

COMMAND REFERENCE 7
Appointment Scheduler 7
Attribute Change 12
Autodialer 13
Calculators 13
Change Drive 14
Clear File 14
Clipboard 15
Commute 16
Compare Disk 23
Compare File 24
Compress 25
Copy Disk 28
Copy File 29
CP Backup 31
Databases 34
Date/Time Stamp Change 41
Delete File 42
Delete Protection 43
DeskConnect 44
Desktop 46
Directory Lock 47
Directory Maintenance 48

- DiskFix 51
- Disk Information 55
- Disk Light 55
- Disk Map 56
- Edit File 57
- Exit PC Shell 58
- Fax Telecommunications 58
- FileFind 61
- FileFix 66
- File Map 67
- Format Data Disk 68
- Help 70
- Hex Edit File 71
- Hide All Lists 73
- Keyboard Macros 73
- Locate File 76
- Make Disk Bootable 78
- Memory Information 79
- Memory Map 79
- Mirror 80
- Modify Display 81
- Modify Program List 84
- Move File 85
- Network Info 86
- Notepads 88
- Outlines 96
- Park Disk Heads 97
- PC-Cache 98
- PCC Config 98
- PC Format 100
- PC Secure 101
- PC Shell 104
- Print 105

Print File List 107
Quick File View 107
Quick Run 107
Recalling Past Commands 108
Remove PC Shell 109
Rename File 109
Rename Volume 110
Run 111
Save Configuration File 112
Screen Blanker 112
Search Disk 113
Search File 114
Setup Configuration 116
Show File Information 118
Size/Move Window 119
Sort Files in Directory 120
Speed Search 121
System Info 122
Telecommunications 123
Undelete File 130
Unformat 134
Utilities 135
Verify Disk 136
Verify File 137
View/Edit Disk 138
View File Contents 140
Virus Defend 141
Wipe 142
Write Protection 145
Zoom the Current Window 146

Index 147

Introduction

PC Tools 7 Quick Reference not only includes the quick reference information you need to manage your computer's disk drives, but also reviews the commands, options, and applications available with PC Tools. This book includes information about working with associated programs such as Desktop, PC-Cache, Mirror, PC-Secure, Commute, and Compress.

Because this book is a quick reference, it is not intended to replace the extensive documentation included with PC Tools. Rather, this book highlights the most frequently used information and reference material that you need to work quickly and efficiently with PC Tools. For example, the documentation includes pages of information explaining how to use scientific formulas on the Desktop's Calculators. This Quick Reference does not repeat that extensive documentation, but tells you how to start the calculator and perform simple calculations.

PC Tools 7 Quick Reference is divided into sections by tasks, applications, and topics. One section, for example, is called "System Info." Suppose that you need to know the number of serial ports connected to and recognized by your computer. You can find that information in the "System Info" section. This section, as well as the others in the book, contains the information that you need to run a command and explains the information displayed on your computer screen.

Now you have essential information at your fingertips with *PC Tools 7 Quick Reference*—and the entire *Que Quick Reference Series*.

GENERAL INFORMATION

PC Tools requires DOS version 3.0 or higher. DOS 3.2 or higher is recommended. To work with Windows, PC Tools requires Microsoft Windows 3.0 or higher.

This book is based on PC Tools Version 7.0.

PC Tools Applications

PC Tools provides a complete set of utilities and a desktop organizer. You can operate these programs in TSR mode by loading them into your computer's memory and using a "hotkey" (a key combination). You also can switch to one of these programs while you work in another application.

The main sections of the package are the following:

COMMUTE	Enables you to run another computer by remote control.
COMPRESS	Organizes the hard disk to increase performance.
DESK CONNECT	Enables easy transfer of programs and files between two computers.
DESKTOP	A complete desktop organizer with nine applications: Notepads, Outlines, Databases, Appointment Scheduler, Telecommunications, Macro Editor, Clipboard, Calculators, and Utilities.
MIRROR/ UNFORMAT	Helps to recover files accidentally erased or disks accidentally formatted or erased.

PC-CACHE   Speeds reading of the disk.

PC FORMAT   Replaces the DOS FORMAT.COM command.

PC SECURE   Enables you to encrypt and decrypt sensitive data.

PC SHELL   Enables easy maintenance of your DOS system, including file, directory, and drive utilities and information.

Caution

Although PC Tools is an easy-to-use program, some of its utilities (if improperly used) could make some of your other programs unusable and prevent your computer from starting. The best procedure is to practice using these utilities on a spare floppy disk and to proceed slowly.

Hints for Using This Book

Because PC Tools consists of many applications in one package, this *Quick Reference* includes under each boxed heading a subheading that refers you to the PC Tools application(s). For example, "PCSHELL" under the heading *Compare Files* tells you that the commands for comparing files are in the PC Shell program.

Some features, such as System Information, are accessible from PC Shell and as stand-alone utilities.

Conventions used in this book

As you read this book, keep in mind the following conventions:

Keys you press and text you type appear in **boldfaced blue** type. The following is a typical entry:

Select the **O**ptions menu by pressing **Alt-O**, then select S**A**ve Configuration.

General Information 3

To select this command, press **Alt-O**, then press **A**.

or

Click the **O**ptions menu, then click the S**A**ve Configuration command.

Combination keys, such as **Alt-O** or **Ctrl-Esc**, indicate that you hold the first key (the **Alt** or **Ctrl** key) while you press the second key. (**Alt** is the Alternate key and **Ctrl** is the Control key.)

The phrase "Click the option" means that you position the mouse cursor on the option and then press and release the mouse button (usually the left button) once.

The phrase "Click and drag the file" means that you position the mouse cursor on the file, then press and hold the mouse button as you slide the mouse to move the file, then release the mouse button.

The phrase "arrow keys" refers to the **up arrow**, **down arrow**, **left arrow**, or **right arrow**. The phrase "cursor keys" refers to **Home**, **End**, **PgUp**, **PgDn**, **up arrow**, **down arrow**, **left arrow**, or **right arrow**.

Using Keyboard Commands

When you first use PC Tools, you may be confused because you can execute many commands in more than one way. This book does not always present the shortest way to execute such commands, but the steps in this book work from anywhere in the program. As you gain experience with PC Tools, you will learn keystroke combinations that enable you to work more quickly.

To select files

1. Select the drive where the files are located by pressing **Ctrl** plus the letter of the drive. For example, to select the A drive, press **Ctrl-A**.

2. Select the directory where the files are stored by pressing **Tab** repeatedly to select the Tree List window. Then use the cursor keys to highlight the directory.

3. Select the files by pressing Tab repeatedly to select the File List window. Then use the cursor keys to highlight each file name. While the file name is highlighted, press Enter.

To select a menu

Press and hold the Alt key. The letter for each menu is highlighted. Press the letter for the menu you want to select. For example, to select the File menu, press Alt-F.

To move between selections

To highlight an option, file, command, or other selection, use the up arrow or down arrow.

To move to the next selection within a dialog box, press Tab. To move to the preceding selection within a dialog box press Shift-Tab.

To cancel commands

To cancel a command or dismiss a dialog box anywhere in PC Tools, press Esc or F3.

PC Shell Keyboard Shortcuts

The following keyboard shortcuts are available from within the PC Shell program:

Key(s)	*Command*
F1	Help
F3	Exit PC Shell
Ctrl-A	Select drive A
Ctrl-B	Select drive B
Ctrl-C	Select drive C
Tab	Switch Windows
Del	Single List Display
Ins	Dual List Display
Ctrl-Enter	Run
Alt-space bar	Size/Move Window

General Information

Using the Mouse with PC Tools

Although you do not need a mouse to use PC Tools, full mouse support is available. Using the mouse makes operating the program faster and easier.

To select a menu using the mouse

Position the mouse cursor on the menu name and click the left button. A pull-down menu appears and displays the options available.

To select a command from a menu using the mouse

1. Position the mouse cursor on the menu. Click and hold the left mouse button.

2. Drag the mouse, scrolling the highlighted selection bar through the commands on the menu.

3. When you locate (highlight) the command you want to use, release the mouse button.

or

1. Position the mouse cursor on the menu and click the left mouse button.

2. Move the mouse cursor to the command you want to use and click the left mouse button.

To select an option using the mouse

Move the mouse cursor to the option and click the left mouse button.

To select files using the mouse

1. Press and hold the right mouse button to produce the highlight bar. Position the highlight bar on the first file you want to select.

2. Press and hold the left mouse button (while holding the right mouse button). Drag the highlight bar over any other files you want to select.

    As you select each file, PC Tools highlights and numbers the file name.

3. Release both mouse buttons after you select all the files you want to use.

To unselect files using the mouse

1. Press the right mouse button and position the highlight bar on the first file you want to unselect.

2. Press and hold the left mouse button. Drag the highlight bar over any other files you want to unselect.

   As you unselect each file, PC Tools removes the highlight and number from the file name.

3. Release both mouse buttons after you unselect all the appropriate files.

To scroll through the File or Tree List using the mouse

1. Move the mouse to the window through which you want to scroll.

2. Press the right mouse button and drag the mouse to the top or bottom of the display to scroll through the list.

Using PC Tools on a Network

You can use PC Tools on a Novell NetWare or IBM Token-Ring Network system, but subtle changes occur. The drives accessible on the network display as additional drive letters on the drive line, which is located under the horizontal menu bar at the top of the screen.

The following commands are not available on a networked drive:

    Directory Sort
    Disk Information
    Disk Map
    File Map
    Format Data Disk
    Make System Disk

Rename Volume
Search Disk
Verify Disk
View/Edit Disk

If you select one of these commands on a networked drive, PC Tools displays a message box telling you that the function is not available on a network.

COMMAND REFERENCE

Following is an alphabetical listing of PC Tools commands and features, including their purposes and the procedures you use to achieve specific results. Some entries also include cautions or notes.

Appointment Scheduler

Beg / Int / Adv   *DESKTOP*

Purpose

An electronic calendar containing a calendar, a to-do list, and a scheduler.

To start the Appointment Scheduler

1. Select the **D**esktop menu by pressing **Alt-D**, then select **A**ppointment Scheduler.

2. Select a file with a TM extension from the Files dialog box.

   The Appointment Scheduler screen appears.

To move around the Appointment Scheduler

Press **Tab** to move between the Monthly Calendar, the Daily Scheduler, and the To-Do sections of the Appointment Scheduler.

or

Move the mouse to the section you want to use and click either mouse button.

To make a new appointment

1. Select the Monthly Calendar by pressing **Tab**.

2. Press the arrow keys to select the date of the appointment. Press **PgUp** or **PgDn** (or click the arrows at the corners of the calendar box) to change months. Press **Ctrl-PgUp** or **Ctrl-PgDn** to change years. Press **Home** to return to today's date.

3. Select the Daily Scheduler by pressing **Tab**.

4. Press the **up arrow** or **down arrow** to change the selected time. Press **PgUp** or **PgDn** (or click the arrows at the corners of the Daily Scheduler box) to scroll through the day's schedule.

5. Press **F10**. From the **A**ppointment menu, select **M**ake New Appointment.

6. Type the description, the starting date, the ending date, the time, and the duration.

7. Select **S**ettings. Select whether to repeat this appointment, and how often. Select whether to set the alarm, and when. Select whether to add a note. To accept the settings, select **O**K. To make these settings the default, select **S**ave.

8. To enter the appointment, select **M**ake by pressing **Alt-M**.

   A musical note symbol to the left of the time indicates that you set an alarm. A double note symbol indicates a repeating appointment. An N indicates that you attached a note to the appointment.

To delete an appointment

1. To select an appointment on the Daily Scheduler, press the **up arrow** or **down arrow** to highlight the appointment.

2. Press **F10**. From the **A**ppointment menu, select **D**elete Appointment.

Command Reference

> If this appointment repeats, select **T**oday to cancel today's appointment only or select **A**ll to cancel all occurrences of the appointment.

3. Select **O**K to confirm the deletion and to remove the appointment from the Daily Scheduler.

To edit an appointment

1. To select an appointment on the Daily Scheduler, press the **up arrow** or **down arrow** to highlight the appointment.

2. Press **F10**. From the **A**ppointment menu, select **E**dit Appointment.

3. Type any changes in the appointment.

To find the next appointment

Press **F10**. From the **A**ppointment menu, select **N**ext Appointment.

To find text in an appointment

1. Press **F10**. From the **A**ppointment menu, select **F**ind Appointment.

2. Type the text you want to find. Press **Enter**.

3. To begin the search, select **F**ind by pressing **Alt-F**. To end the search, select **C**ancel by pressing **Alt-C**.

To find free time

1. Press **F10**. From the **A**ppointment menu, select Free **T**ime.

2. Type the start and end times of the range of times you want to search.

3. Press **Tab** to select Any Day or Work Day.

4. Enter the duration of time you want to find.

5. To begin the search, select **F**ind by pressing **Alt-F**.

To see the weekly schedule

Press **F5**.

To show time usage

Press **F8**.

The Show Time command displays seven days at a glance. Dashes indicate appointments, spaces indicate free times, and dots indicate potential conflicts.

Press **F8** again to return to the main window of the Appointment Scheduler.

To attach notes

1. To select an appointment on the Daily Scheduler, press the **up arrow** or **down arrow** to highlight the appointment.

2. Press **F10**. From the **A**ppointment menu, select **A**ttach Note.

3. Type the text of the note.

4. Press **F10**. From the **F**ile menu, select **S**ave. Type the file name, then press **Enter**. Select **S**ave, then **Esc**.

To make a to-do list entry

1. Press **F10**. From the **T**o-Do menu, select **M**ake.

2. Type the to-do entry.

3. Enter the Start Date, the End Date, and a priority number. To attach a note, select **A**ttach Note.

4. Select **M**ake to make the entry.

To delete a to-do entry

1. Select the to-do entry you want to delete.

2. Press **F10**. From the **T**o-Do menu, select **D**elete To-Do Entry.

To change appointment settings

1. Press **F10**. From the **C**ontrols menu, select **A**ppointment Settings.

2. Select settings in the Appointment Settings dialog box.

3. Press **O**K to accept the new settings.

Command Reference

To set holiday settings

1. Press **F10**. From the **C**ontrols menu, select **N**ational Holiday Settings or **U**ser Holiday Settings.

2. Select the holidays.

3. Press **O**K to add the selected holidays.

To change the screen layout

1. Press **F10**. From the **C**ontrols menu, select **S**chedule Layouts.

2. Select a layout style.

3. Select **O**K.

To load files

1. Press **F10**. From the **F**ile menu, select **L**oad.

2. Select a file from the Files Load dialog box. Press **Enter**.

To save files

1. Press **F10**. From the **F**ile menu, select **S**ave.

2. To change the file name, type the new name. Press **Enter**.

3. Select **S**ave to save the file.

To print

1. Press **F10**. From the **F**ile menu, select **P**rint.

2. Select Today Only, This Week, This Month, or This Year.

3. To specify a schedule layout, select **L**ayout. Select the type of form and print layout. Select **O**K.

4. Select **P**rint to start the printing.

To use the autosave feature

1. Press **F10**. From the **F**ile menu, select **A**utosave.

2. Enter the number of minutes you want to elapse between each automatic save.

3. Press **Tab** to select the automatic save options. Use the **up arrow** and **down arrow** to select On or Off.

4. Select **OK** to set the automatic save feature.

Notes

When you run PC Tools Desktop as a memory-resident program, you can add, delete, or change appointments, even when you are working in another program.

Using macros tied to the Appointment Scheduler alarm, the computer can run programs even when you are not present.

Attribute Change

Int / Adv   *PCSHELL*

Purpose

Enables you to view and change a file's attributes and date and time stamp.

To change file attributes or the date/time stamp

1. Select the file(s) whose attributes or date/time stamp you want to change.

2. Select the **F**ile menu by pressing **Alt-F**, then select Chan**G**e File.

3. Select **A**ttribute Change.

4. Select **A**rchive, **R**ead Only, **H**idden, or **S**ystem to toggle the attribute on or off.

5. Select the Date or Time field and type the new date or time.

6. Select **U**pdate to save the changes to the disk and return to the main PC Shell screen.

Caution

Do not change the attributes of system files or copy-protected files or you may prevent your computer programs from working properly.

Command Reference   13

Autodialer

Beg / Int / Adv   **DESKTOP**

Purpose

Enables you (automatically) to dial a phone number that appears on your computer screen.

To dial with Autodialer

1. Display the phone number on-screen. (You can type it at the DOS prompt.)

2. Press the Autodialer hotkey (the default is **Ctrl-O**).

   A dialog box containing the number appears.

3. Select an option:

   Dial dials the phone number.

   Next searches for the next phone number on-screen.

   Cancel cancels the autodialer.

Notes

You must have a Hayes-compatible modem connected to your computer.

Desktop must be memory-resident. See *Desktop* for details.

The Autodialer must be configured from the Databases application of Desktop. See *Databases* for details.

Calculators

Beg / Int / Ad   **DESKTOP**

Purpose

PC Tools Desktop has four calculators: algebraic, financial, programmer's, and scientific.

To start a calculator

From the main **D**esktop menu, select **C**alculators, then select the calculator you want to use.

To use the calculators

The algebraic calculator works like a regular calculator.

The financial calculator performs calculations pertaining to interest on IRAs, loan and mortgage repayment, and depreciation.

The programmer's calculator expresses calculations in hex, octal, binary, and decimal.

The scientific calculator performs functions such as sine, cosine, and tangent.

Change Drive

Beg / Int / Adv   *PCSHELL, DM*

Purpose

Enables you to change the drive accessed by PC Shell.

To change the current drive

Press **Ctrl** plus the letter of the drive. For example, to select drive A, press **Ctrl-A**.

To change the current drive using the mouse

Click the new drive on the drive line (the second line of your screen).

Clear File

Int / Adv   *PCSHELL, WIPE*

Purpose

Deletes the selected file(s) and writes the same byte pattern in every cluster that the file occupied, removing any data contained in the file.

Command Reference   15

To clear a file

1. Select the file(s) you want to clear.

2. Select the **F**ile menu by pressing **Alt-F**, then select Chan**G**e File.

3. Select **C**lear File.

4. To clear the selected files, select **W**ipe.

Caution

Unlike the DOS DELETE command, files erased using the **C**lear File command cannot be undeleted. Use **C**lear File only if you are sure you will never want the file again.

Clipboard

Beg / Int / Adv   *DESKTOP*

Purpose

Enables you to copy and paste text from one DOS application to another.

To use the Clipboard

Before using the Clipboard, run Desktop in TSR mode. For more information, see *Desktop*.

To copy text to the Clipboard

1. Press **Ctrl-space bar** to enter the Desktop, then select Clip**B**oard. Press **F10**. From the **C**opy/Paste menu, select **C**opy To Clipboard.

   or

   Press **Ctrl-Del**.

2. Position the cursor at the beginning of the block of text you want to copy into the Clipboard.

3. Press **Enter**.

4. Press the arrow keys to mark the block of text you want to copy into the Clipboard.

   The cursor changes to a block cursor.

5. Press **Enter** to copy the marked text.

   The text remains in the Clipboard until you replace it or end the program.

To paste text from the Clipboard

1. Position the cursor where you want to paste the text from the Clipboard.

2. Press **Ctrl-space bar** to enter the Desktop, then select Clip**B**oard. Press **F10**. From the **C**opy/Paste menu, select **P**aste From Clipboard.

   or

   Press **Ctrl-Ins**.

To edit text in the Clipboard

1. Press **Ctrl-space bar** to enter the Desktop, then select Clip**B**oard.

2. Select **E**dit.

3. Edit the text. You can use the **E**rase Block, **M**ark or **U**nmark Block, **D**elete All Text, **I**nsert File, or **G**oto commands in addition to the regular cursor-movement keys.

Commute

Beg/Int/Adv   *COMMUTE*

Purpose

Enables one PC to run another by remote control. The controlling computer can transfer files, run programs, operate Windows, and perform other functions on either machine. You can use scripts to automate the entire process.

To start Commute

1. At the DOS command line, type **COMMUTE** and press **Enter**.

2. Type a User Name, then press **Enter**. Select **OK**.

Command Reference

3. Select the type of connection, then select **O**K.

   Select **M**odem if the computers are connected by telephone lines and modems.

   > If you select **M**odem, select the type of modem. If your modem is not on the list, select the Hayes or Hayes-compatible modem with the same speed as your modem.
   >
   > Select **O**K.
   >
   > Select the COM port where the modem is connected.
   >
   > Select **O**K.

   Select **L**AN if the computers are connected by a Novell LAN.

   Select **D**irect Connection if the computers are connected by a null-modem cable.

   > If you select **D**irect Connection, select the COM port where the null-modem cable is connected.
   >
   > Select **O**K.

   If necessary, you can change the connection type later.

To wait for a call (on the computer giving control)

1. Select Wait For **A**ny Caller from the Call Manager window.

2. Select **O**K.

   Commute returns to DOS so the user can work while the computer waits for a call.

   If another computer calls, a dialog box appears. To accept the call, press any key except **Esc**. To reject the call, press **Esc**. If you do not press a key within 10 seconds, the calling PC takes control of the PC.

   When the calling PC takes control, the controlled computer's Scroll Lock light blinks.

To call and take control

1. Select Call And **T**ake Control from the Call Manager window.

   The Private Call List appears.

2. Select the PC you want to call, then select **O**K.

To call and give control to another PC

1. Select Wait For **A**ny Caller from the Call Manager window.

   The computer exits to DOS leaving part of Commute resident in memory.

2. Select Call Manager by pressing **Alt-RShift** (hold **Alt** and press the **Right Shift** key).

   or

   Run Commute again.

3. Select Call And **G**ive Control.

4. Select a PC from the list, then select **O**K.

   A Commute Call In Progress dialog box appears showing the status of the call.

To look at your PC (on the controlling computer)

1. Select Session Manager by pressing **Alt-RShift** (hold **Alt** and press the **Right Shift** key).

2. Select **L**ook At Your PC.

   You now see the controlling computer's display and use the controlling computer's files and commands.

3. To return to the Commute session, type **EXIT**, then press **Enter**.

To send files to your PC (to the controlling computer)

1. Select Session Manager by pressing **Alt-RShift** (hold **Alt** and press the **Right Shift** key).

2. Select **G**et Files From Other PC.

   The Get Files From Other PC dialog box appears.

3. Type the path and file name of the file(s) you want to get from the controlled PC, then press **Enter**. You can use wildcards and exclusions (with the minus sign) in file names.

4. Type the path of the controlling PC's target directory, then press **Enter**.

5. Select any file transfer options:

   Compress **F**iles compresses each file before sending it and decompresses each file before saving it.

   Automatic O**V**erwrite enables you to overwrite a file with the same name in the target directory. If this option is off, a dialog box appears when a file is about to be overwritten. Select this option when using an Auto-Call script.

   Disable Virus Checking specifies whether to scan each file for viruses before sending it. If this option is off, a dialog box appears when a virus is detected. Select this option when using an Auto-Call script.

   Include **S**ubdirectories enables you to transfer matching files in subdirectories of the entered path (if you use DOS wildcard characters).

   Copy Only If **A**rchive Bit Set copies only those files whose archive bit is set. This option is useful if you use Commute to back up one computer's files to another computer.

   Clear Archive **B**it After Copy clears the archive bit after copying a file. This option is useful if you use Commute to back up one computer's files to another computer.

   Copy **N**ewer Files Only copies each file only if the file is newer than the file of the same name in the target directory. If this option is on, Automatic O**V**erwrite is ignored.

6. Select **O**K.

To send files to the other PC (to the controlled computer)

1. Select Session Manager by pressing **Alt-RShift** (hold **Alt** and press the **Right Shift** key).

2. Select **S**end Files To Other PC.

   The Send Files To Other PC dialog box appears.

3. Type the path and file name of the file(s) you want to send to the controlling PC, then press **Enter**. You can use wildcards (such as **?** or *****) and exclusions (with the minus sign) in file names.

4. Type the path of the controlled PC's target directory, then press **Enter**.

5. Select any file transfer options:

   Compress **F**iles
   Automatic O**V**erwrite
   Disable Virus Checking
   Include **S**ubdirectories
   Copy Only If **A**rchive Bit Set
   Clear Archive **B**it After Copy
   Copy **N**ewer Files Only

6. Select **O**K.

To chat with the other PC user (on either computer)

1. Select Session Manager by pressing **Alt-RShift** (hold **Alt** and press the **Right Shift** key).

2. Select **C**hat With Other PC.

   The Chat window appears.

3. Type your comments in the Chat window. Your comments appear in the window along with those of the other user.

4. To close the Chat window, press **Esc**.

To add an entry to the Private Call List

1. Select **P**rivate Call List from the **F**ile menu.

   The Private Call List appears.

2. Select **N**ew by pressing **Alt-N**.

   The Edit Call List dialog box appears.

3. Enter information about the PCs you want to call.

================================ Command Reference

This information can include the following:

Private Name
Connect By...
Phone Number
Password

4. To close the Edit Call List dialog box, select **O**K.

5. To close the Private Call List, select **O**K.

To edit an entry in the Private Call List

1. Select **P**rivate Call List from the **F**ile menu.

   The Private Call List appears.

2. Select an entry from the list.

3. Select **E**dit.

   The Edit Call List dialog box appears.

4. Edit information in that entry. Select **O**K.

5. To close the Private Call List, select **O**K.

To delete an entry from the Private Call List

1. Select **P**rivate Call List from the **F**ile menu.

   The Private Call List appears.

2. Select an entry from the list.

3. Select **D**elete.

To use advanced options

1. Select Session Manager by pressing **Alt-RShift** (hold **Alt** and press the **Right Shift** key).

2. Select **A**dvanced Options.

3. Select **P**rint Direction.

4. Select the options you want to use:

   Re**B**oot Other PC
   Lock Other Keyboard
   Print Direction
   Redraw Your Screen
   Save Current Screen

5. Select **O**K.

To change the configuration options

1. Select Session Manager by pressing **Alt-RShift** (hold **Alt** and press the **Right Shift** key).

   or

   Run Commute again.

2. Select the **C**onfigure menu by pressing **Alt-C** or by pressing **F10**, **C**.

3. Select the configuration options you want to change:

   Hot**K**ey
   Modem List
   COM Port
   Baud Rate
   Connection **T**ype
   Sc**H**edule Calls
   Auto-Call Scripts

To save your configuration

1. Select the **C**onfigure menu by pressing **Alt-C** or by pressing **F10**, **C**.

2. Select **S**ave Configuration.

To end a Commute session (on the controlling computer)

1. Select Session Manager by pressing **Alt-RShift** (hold **Alt** and press the **Right Shift** key).

2. Select **E**nd The Session.

   Your PC (the controlling computer) is disconnected from the other PC. The other PC continues to wait for calls until Commute is unloaded from memory.

3. Select **O**K.

To unload Commute from memory (on the controlled computer)

1. Select Session Manager by pressing **Alt-RShift** (hold **Alt** and press the **Right Shift** key).

2. Select **U**nload From Memory.

   or

   At the DOS command line, type **KILL** and press **Enter**. (Warning: KILL also unloads other utilities loaded into memory, such as PC Shell.)

   or

   At the DOS command line, type **COMMUTE /U** and press **Enter**.

   The other PC (the controlled computer) is disconnected from the controlling PC.

Note

Both computers must run Commute. The two computers must be physically joined by telephone lines and modem, by Novell LAN, or by a null-modem cable. With simple scripts, file transfers and commands can run automatically.

Compare Disk

Beg / Int / Adv   *PCSHELL*

Purpose

Enables you to determine whether two disks are identical. The source and target disks must be in the same format.

To compare disks

1. Select the **D**isk menu by pressing **Alt-D**, then select C**O**mpare.

2. Select the source drive from the Disk Compare dialog box by using the arrow keys. Press **Enter**, then select **OK**.

   or

   Click the source drive in the Disk Compare dialog box.

3. Select the target drive from the Disk Compare dialog box by using the arrow keys. Press **Enter**, then select **O**K.

   or

   Click the target drive in the Disk Compare dialog box.

4. Insert the source disk and select **O**K.

5. Depending on your hardware configuration, the Disk Compare dialog box may prompt you to insert the target disk. Insert the target disk and select **O**K.

6. During the disk compare process, the following letters may appear in the Disk Compare dialog box:

   R   Reading track

   C   Comparing track

   When a dot appears in the track, that track has been compared to the target disk.

7. To return to the main PC Shell menu, select **C**ancel.

Compare File

Beg / Int / Adv   *PCSHELL*

Purpose

Enables you to determine whether two files are identical. The files can be in any directories, on the same disk, on different disks, and in different drives. The files can have different or matching file names. You also can compare several sets of files at one time.

To compare files

1. Select the first file or set of files you want to compare.

2. Select the **F**ile menu by pressing **Alt-F**, then select Comp**A**re.

3. Select the drive that holds the second file or set of files you want to compare. Select **O**K.

Command Reference

4. Select **M**atching Names or **D**ifferent Names.
5. Select the directory of the second file or set of files you want to compare.
6. If you selected **D**ifferent Names, type the name and extension of the file(s) you want to compare. Select **O**K.
7. Select Co**M**pare.

   If the files are different, PC Tools displays the sector and offset (the position within the sector) and the ASCII value of the difference.

   Select **O**K to continue the comparison. If you selected more than one file, Compare continues with each in turn.

   After all files have been compared, select **O**K.

   PC Shell returns to the main screen.

Compress

Beg / Int / Adv *COMPRESS*

Purpose

Stores the parts of each file together. (When DOS saves files to your disk, it randomly places the parts of each file. Compress rearranges the disk, moving the parts of each file to a contiguous location so that the computer can read the files more quickly.)

To start Compress

Before running Compress, remove all memory-resident programs, including caches.

Type **COMPRESS** at the DOS prompt and press **Enter**.

To view disk statistics

1. Press **F10**. From the **A**nalysis menu, select **D**isk Statistics.

   The Disk Statistics dialog box displays information about the disk and suggests a compression technique.

If the disk contains any cross-linked file chains, unattached file clusters, or bad clusters within file chains, run DiskFix before compressing the disk (see *DiskFix* for details).

2. Select **O**K.

To view the file fragmentation analysis

1. Press **F10**. From the **A**nalysis menu, select **F**ile Fragmentation Analysis.

   The File Fragmentation Analysis dialog box displays information about possible fragmentation of files on the disk.

2. After reviewing the information, select **C**ancel.

To sort directories

1. Press **F10**. From the **O**ptions menu, select File **S**ort Options.

   or

   Press **F9**.

2. Select the file characteristic by which you want to sort:

   Date/**T**ime
   File Name
   Extension
   Size

3. Select how you want to sort the files by the characteristic:

   No Sorting
   Ascending
   Descending

4. Select **O**K.

To set ordering options

1. Press **F10**. From the **O**ptions menu, select **O**rdering Methods.

Command Reference

2. Select one of the following options:

   Standard places directories first, then places files as specified by Compress. This option is the fastest way to order the files.

   File Placement places directories first, then places files as specified by the user, then places COM and EXE files, then places any other files.

   Directories First places directories first, then places files by directory. This option maximizes hard disk performance.

   D**I**rectories With Files places each directory with its files.

To select the compression technique

1. Press **F10**. From the **O**ptions menu, select **C**ompression Technique.

2. Select one of the following compression options:

   Optimize **D**irectories moves directories to the front of the disk, but does not unfragment files.

   O**P**timize Free Space moves all directories and files to the front of the disk, but does not unfragment files.

   Unfragment Files unfragments files, but does not move files to the front of the disk.

   Full Optimization unfragments files, arranges the directories and files as specified in the **O**ptions menu, then moves them to the front of the disk.

   Full Optimization With **C**lear is the same as **F**ull Optimization, but also clears empty space at the end of the disk.

   File **S**ort rearranges file names in directories as specified in the **O**ptions menu, but does not move or unfragment the files.

To generate a report before compression

1. Press **F10**. From the **O**ptions menu, select **P**rint Report.

This command generates a report (in a file called COMPRESS.PRT) that indicates the time needed to run the program; the options selected; and the number of used, unused, and bad clusters on the disk.

2. Select whether to send the report to **P**rinter or **D**isk.

To begin compression

1. Press **F10**. From the **C**ompress menu, select **B**egin Compress.

2. Select **O**K.

   The Compress display shows a map of the disk as it is compressed (indicating the reading and writing of clusters), the elapsed time, and percentage of the task completed.

   When the compression is finished, the program asks whether you want to run Mirror (see *Mirror*).

3. Reboot your computer.

Caution

Do not run Compress from Windows.

Note

Compress does not work on network servers or drives.

Copy Disk

Beg / Int / Adv   *PCSHELL*

Purpose

Copies standard DOS floppy disks. The source and target disks must be the same format.

To copy a disk

1. Select the **D**isk menu by pressing **Alt-D**, then select **C**opy.

2. Select the source drive from the Disk Copy dialog box. Select **O**K.

3. Select the target drive from the Disk Copy dialog box. Select **OK**.

4. Insert the source disk into the correct drive.

5. If prompted, insert the target disk into the correct drive. Make sure the target disk is not copy-protected.

6. Select **OK**.

   During the disk copy process, the following letters may appear in the Disk Copy dialog box:

   F   Formatting track

   R   Reading track

   W   Writing track

   When a dot appears in the track, that track has been copied successfully to the target disk. After the disk is copied, PC Shell returns to the main screen.

Caution

The Copy Disk command formats the target disk as the program copies to the disk. Any files already on the target disk are lost when you use the Copy Disk command. Be sure that the target disk contains no important files before you start this command. To copy files to the target disk without destroying files already on the disk, use the Copy File command.

Copy File

Beg / Int / Adv   *PCSHELL*

Purpose

Enables you to copy one or more files to the same drive with a different file name, to another directory on the same drive, or to another drive.

To copy files

1. Select the file(s) you want to copy by using the arrow keys to highlight each file name. Press **Enter** to select each file.

2. Select the **F**ile menu by pressing **Alt-F**, then select **C**opy.

   or

   Press **F5**.

   If you are using the Dual File List display (which is selectable from the **V**iew menu), PC Shell displays the following message:

   ```
   Confirm using second path as target.
   ```

   If the other window is the one where you want to copy the files, select **O**K. A dialog box appears, and the files are copied. If you do not want to copy the files to the other window, select **N**o.

3. Select the target drive in the File Copy box using the **up arrow** or **down arrow**. Select **O**K to continue.

4. If the target drive contains subdirectories, select the directory where you want to copy the file(s) and press **Enter**.

5. If the target drive contains files with the same names as the files being copied, select one of the following options:

   Replace **A**ll replaces all files in the target directory with the remaining files of the same names in the source directory.

   Replace File replaces the current file in the target directory with the file of the same name in the source directory.

   Skip **F**ile skips to the next file to be copied (does not copy the current file).

   Skip All skips all the remaining files to be copied and returns to the main PC Shell screen.

   Cancel returns to the main PC Shell screen.

   If you are copying a file into the same directory, a Copy dialog box appears. Type a new file name, select OK, then select Co**P**y.

   The files are copied to the target directory. A Copy dialog box is displayed as the file(s) are copied.

Command Reference

When the copying is complete, you return to the main PC Shell screen.

To copy files using the mouse
1. Select the file(s) you want to copy.
2. In the File menu, click Copy.
3. Click the target drive in the drive line.
4. Click the target subdirectory.

CP Backup

Beg / Int / Adv **CPBACKUP**

Purpose

Makes a backup copy of the contents of your hard disk. (CP Backup is a separate utility program included with PC Tools.)

To activate CP Backup
1. Type **CPBACKUP** at the DOS prompt and press **Enter**.
2. Answer the questions to configure CP Backup. This configuration determines what type of disk drives and tape drives are available for backing up your hard drive.

To back up your hard drive
1. Select Backup from the main menu.
2. Select Backup FRom by pressing **Alt-R**.
3. Select the drive you want to back up by using the **up arrow** and **down arrow**, then press the **space bar**.
4. Select Backup To by pressing **Alt-T**.
5. Select the drive to which you want to back up by using the **up arrow** and **down arrow**, then press **Enter**.
6. Select Start Backup by pressing **Alt-S**.

Type the name of the backup, then press **Enter**.

7. Select **O**K by pressing **Alt-O**.

To restore data to your hard drive

1. Select **R**estore from the main menu.

2. Select Restore F**R**om by pressing **Alt-R**.

3. Select the drive you want to restore by using the **up arrow** and **down arrow**, then press the **space bar**.

4. Select Restore **T**o by pressing **Alt-T**.

5. Select the drive to which you want to restore by using the **up arrow** and **down arrow** keys, then press **Enter**.

6. Select **S**tart Restore by pressing **Alt-S**.

7. During Restore, CP Backup may find the original file on your hard drive. If you selected Overwrite Warning in the **O**ptions menu, CP Backup displays a warning dialog box. Select O**V**erwrite, Overwrite With **N**ewer File Only, or **S**kip This File.

8. Select **O**K.

To select specific files to back up

1. Select the **O**ptions menu by pressing **Alt-O**, then select **S**election Options.

2. Select options:

   S**U**bdirectory Inclusion selects or deselects the subdirectories when you select or deselect a directory.

   Include/Exclude Files enables you to type file specifications, including DOS wildcard characters **?** and ***** and the exclusion symbol (**–**). For example, the entry **?.* –*.BAK** specifies all files whose file name is a single character (?.) with any extension (*) except files with the BAK extension (–*.BAK).

   Attribute Exclusion enables you to select the attributes you want to exclude.

   Date Range Selection enables you to specify the range of dates for which you want to back up files.

3. Press **Esc** to continue.

Command Reference

To select a backup method

1. Select the **O**ptions menu by pressing **Alt-O**, then select **B**ackup Method.

2. Select the method you want to use:

    Full backs up all selected files in all selected directories and clears archive bits of backed up files.

    Incremental backs up only those files whose archive bits are set and appends this backup to the end of the last full backup.

    Differential backs up only those files that have changed since the last full backup does not change archive bits.

    F**U**ll Copy is the same as **F**ull, but does not change archive bits.

    Separate Incremental is similar to **I**ncremental, but backs up only those files changed or created since the last backup and is not appended to the end of the full backup. This method also clears archive bits.

    If you selected a tape drive as a backup medium, the following additional options may be available:

    Full/Erase Tape is a full backup to tape, with the option of overwriting previous backups on tape.

    Full/Append to Tape is a full backup to tape, with the option of starting a new backup immediately after the last backup on the tape.

3. Select **O**K.

To scan for viruses

1. Select the **O**ptions menu by pressing **Alt-O**.

2. Select Vir**U**s Detection.

To display an overwrite warning

1. Select the **O**ptions menu by pressing **Alt-O**.

2. Select **O**verwrite Warning.

To save a setup

1. Select the **F**ile menu by pressing **Alt-F**, then select Save Setup **A**s.

2. Type a name for this configuration (without a file extension). Press **Enter**.

   3. Select **O**K.

To load a previously saved setup

   1. Select the **F**ile menu by pressing **Alt-F**, then select **L**oad Setup.

   2. Select the setup file you want to use.

   3. Select **O**K.

Notes

Use the same version of CP Backup to back up and restore.

High Speed Direct Memory Access (DMA) makes your Backup run faster, but this feature works only when you back up files to floppy disks. If you use DMA, you cannot use the standard DOS DIR command. To see the directory listing of files on a disk on which you used DMA, use the utility CPBDIR.COM. Windows Backup can run in the background in 386 enhanced mode.

Databases

Beg / Int / Adv   *DESKTOP*

Purpose

The PC Tools Desktop includes a powerful database program. If you use the Desktop as a memory-resident program, you can access Databases to locate phone numbers, clients' names and addresses, or any other information in the databases.

Databases guidelines

When working with PC Tools Databases, remember the following guidelines:

- You can have as many as 15 windows open at one time (with one database per window).

- A field can have no more than 70 characters. A record can have no more than 128 fields and 4,000 characters. A database can have no more than 10,000 records.

- The memo field in dBASE III and dBASE IV is ignored by Databases.

- Databases uses the DBF extension for files containing database information. The DBF files are compatible with dBASE III and dBASE IV.

- Record files, identified with the REC extension, are used by Databases only to maintain information about how to display the database and are not compatible with dBASE III and dBASE IV.

- Form files, identified with the FOR extension, are standard Notepads files.

- Working with Databases can be confusing if you do not know what a database is, what it does, and how it works. You should understand the difference between fields, structure, files, characters, records, and other important database terms.

To create a new database

1. From the main **D**esktop menu, select **D**atabases.

2. Type the file name of the database and select **N**ew by pressing **Alt-N**.

3. Type the field name in the Field Name text box in the Field Editor dialog box.

   You can use any letter, number or the underscore character (_). Use the underscore character to separate words (you cannot use spaces or a blank field name). Field names can be no longer than 10 characters. Lowercase letters are converted to uppercase.

4. Select the Field Type: Character, Numeric, Logical, or Date. Press **Enter**.

   A Character field can contain any letters (A-Z), numbers (0-9) that are used for identification, special symbols (#, $, *, &), spaces, and the underscore character (_). All character fields must have at least one character.

If you copy records from dBASE III or dBASE IV, information longer than 70 characters is not copied.

A Numeric field can contain any number or value that is used in mathematical computations and the decimal point (.), plus sign (+), or minus sign (−) associated with a number. (The + and − signs are optional at the beginning of a number.)

The position of the decimal is fixed after you set it, so numeric fields displayed in columns have aligned decimal points. You can enter up to 19 characters per numeric field. The default numeric field is 0.

PC Tools Desktop Databases does not perform computations within the database, but you can store values in numeric fields for use in dBASE III or dBASE IV.

A Logical field can contain a single character representing a true or false condition in a database. True is defined as T, t, Y, or y. False is defined as F, f, N, or n. A logical field divides the contents of a database file into two groups: one for which the condition is true and another for which the condition is false. The default logical field is F.

A Date field always contains eight characters that store numeric codes for the month, day, and year in the format MM/DD/YY. (Date fields always assume the Twentieth century.) The default date field is 00/00/00.

You can use Date fields as dates in data manipulation only. You cannot use PC Tools Databases date fields in dBASE III or dBASE IV formulas.

5. Type the field size and press **Enter**. Size limits of fields vary according to the field type:

   Character   Maximum of 70 characters, minimum of 1 character.

   Logical   Always one character.

   Date   Always 8 characters.

   Numeric   Maximum of 19 characters.

Command Reference

Type the number of decimal places (if applicable) and press **Enter**.

6. Select **A**dd.

7. Repeat steps 3 through 6 to add additional fields.

8. To save the new database and close the dialog box, select **S**ave. Be sure to save the database structure before you add records to the database.

   The field definitions appear in the default form.

   To cancel the database creation and return to the Desktop menu without saving the database, select **C**ancel or press **Esc**.

To add a new record

1. Press **F10**. From the **F**ile menu, select **M**odify Data.

2. Press **F10**. From the **E**dit menu, select **A**dd New Record.

3. Move the cursor to the appropriate field and type the new information. The default mode is Overtype. To switch to Insert mode, press **Ins**.

To edit existing records

1. Press **F10**. From the **F**ile menu, select **M**odify Data.

2. Select the record you want to edit.

3. Use the cursor keys to move to any field in that record.

4. Type the new information or edit the existing information. Press **Enter**.

5. Repeat steps 2 through 4 to edit additional fields.

To delete a record

1. Press **F10**. From the **F**ile menu, select **M**odify Data.

2. Select the record you want to mark for deletion.

3. Press **F10**. From the **E**dit menu, select **D**elete Record.

   The **D**elete Record command marks the record for deletion. The record is not deleted until you run **P**ack Database.

A database must have at least one record. If you attempt to delete the last record, a warning appears.

To restore deleted records

1. Press **F10**. From the **F**ile menu, select **M**odify Data.

2. Press **F10**. From the **E**dit menu, select **U**ndelete Records.

   The **U**ndelete Records command unmarks all records marked for deletion.

   You cannot select individual records for undeletion, and you cannot undelete records after running **P**ack Database.

To pack records

1. Press **F10**. From the **F**ile menu, select **M**odify Data.

2. Press **F10**. From the **E**dit menu, select **P**ack Database. A warning appears. Select **O**K to continue.

   The **P**ack Database command deletes all records that you marked for deletion with **D**elete Record.

To hide a record

1. Select the record you want to hide.

2. Press **F10**. From the **E**dit menu, select **H**ide Current Record.

To select records

1. Press **F10**. From the **E**dit menu, select Select **R**ecords.

2. In the Select Records dialog box, type the names of the fields you want to use to select records. Press **Enter**.

3. Type the field criteria you want to use to match a specified field. Press **Enter**.

4. To choose **S**elect, press **Alt-S**.

To select all records

Press **F10**. From the **E**dit menu, choose Se**L**ect All Records.

Command Reference

To edit field names

1. Press **F10**. From the **F**ile menu, select **M**odify Data.

2. Press **F10**. From the **E**dit menu, select **E**dit Fields.

3. To edit the fields, select any option in the Field Editor. Make the changes, then press **Enter**.

4. To record the changes, select **A**dd by pressing **Alt-A**.

5. To save the edited changes, select **S**ave by pressing **Alt-S**.

To sort the database

1. Press **F10**. From the **E**dit menu, select **S**ort Database.

2. Select the fields you want to sort from the Sort Field Select dialog box. Select **N**ext or **P**rev to select the next or preceding field.

3. To sort according to the selected field, select **S**ort by pressing **Alt-S**.

To find text in all fields

1. Press **F10**. From the **S**earch menu, select **F**ind Text In All Fields.

2. Type the text you want to find. Press **Enter**.

3. Press **Tab** or use the **up arrow** or **down arrow** to select Search All Records, Search Selected Records, or Search from Current Record.

4. To select **S**earch, press **Alt-S**.

To go to a record

1. Press **F10**. From the **S**earch menu, select **G**oto Record.

2. In the Goto Record dialog box, type the number of the record to which you want to go. Press **Enter**.

3. To select **G**oto, press **Alt-G**.

To create a new form

1. Press **F10**. From the **D**esktop menu, select **N**otepads.

2. Type the name of the new form.

Use a name other than the name of the database. Be sure to name the new form with a FOR extension.

3. To create a new file, select **OK**.
4. Type the text using the Notepads functions.

   Enclose all field names in brackets ([ ]).
5. Press **F10**. From the **F**ile menu, select **S**ave to save the Notepads file.
6. Press **Alt-S** to save the form.
7. Press **Esc**.

To load forms

1. Press **F10**. From the **F**ile menu, select **L**oad.
2. Select the form you want to load from the Load Form dialog box. (Forms must have the FOR extension.)
3. Press **Alt-L** to load the form.

To print

1. Press **F10**. From the **F**ile menu, select **P**rint.
2. Select the printer port, number of copies, line spacing, and starting page number.
3. Select **P**rint by pressing **Alt-P**.

To set the page layout

1. Press **F10**. From the **C**ontrols menu, select **P**age Layout.
2. Set the margins and paper size.
3. Select **O**K by pressing **Alt-O**.

To configure Autodial

1. Load an existing database or create a new database.
2. Press **F10**. From the **C**ontrols menu, select **C**onfigure Autodial.
3. Set the dial (either tone or pulse), port, baud rate, and any access and long distance codes.
4. Select **O**K by pressing **Alt-O**.

To use Autodial

To use Autodial, you must have a Hayes-compatible modem connected to your computer.

1. Select the record containing the phone number you want to dial.
2. Press **F10**. From the **C**ontrols menu, select **A**utodial.
3. Pick up the telephone.
4. Wait until the phone begins to ring, then press **Esc** to disconnect the modem.

To save a setup

Press **F10**. From the **C**ontrols menu, select **S**ave setup.

Date/Time Stamp Change

Int / Adv *PCSHELL*

Purpose

Enables you to view and change the date and time that DOS stamps on the file.

To change the date/time stamp

1. Select the file(s) whose date/time stamp you want to change.
2. Select the **F**ile menu by pressing **Alt-F**, then select Chan**G**e File.
3. Select **A**ttribute Change.
4. Select the Date or Time field and type the new date or time.
5. Select **U**pdate to save the changes to the disk and return to the main PC Shell screen.

Delete File

Int / Adv   *PCSHELL*

Purpose

Enables you to delete or erase a file or files, including files with Hidden, Read-only, or System attributes.

To delete a file

1. Select the file(s) you want to delete.

2. Select the **F**ile menu by pressing **Alt-F**, then select **D**elete File.

3. The File Delete dialog box displays the current file name and extension. Select one of the following options:

   Delete   Deletes the currently selected file.

   Next File   Skips the currently selected file and displays the next file.

   Delete **A**ll   Deletes all the selected files.

   Cancel   Stops deleting files and returns to the main PC Shell screen.

   If you select only one file, only **D**elete and **C**ancel are available in the File Delete dialog box.

Note

When you delete a file using this command, PC Tools (and other programs) can undelete the file and recover the data. If you do not want the file to be recoverable, use the **C**lear File command.

Delete Protection

Beg / Int / Adv   *DATAMON*

Purpose

Provides two methods to prevent accidental deletion of files. Delete Sentry saves deleted files in a hidden directory named \SENTRY. You can use Delete Sentry on local or network drives. Delete Tracker saves information that can help to recover deleted files.

To turn on Delete Sentry

1. Select **D**elete Protection.

2. Select Delete **S**entry. Select **O**K.

3. Specify which files you want Sentry to save:

    All Files   Saves all deleted files.

    Only **S**pecified Files   Saves only those files that match your specifications.

    Enter file name specifications in the Include and Exclude boxes, using DOS wildcard characters ***** and **?**. For example, to save all files except backup files, enter ***.*** in the Include box and ***.BAK** in the Exclude box.

4. Turn on or off Do **N**ot Save Archived Files. If this option is on, Delete Sentry saves only files whose archive bit is not set; if off, Delete Sentry saves files regardless of their archive bit.

5. Enter the number of days after which you want to purge (remove) a deleted file from the hidden directory. You can purge any file from this directory manually at any time by using **U**ndelete.

6. Specify the maximum percentage of the hard disk reserved for the hidden directory. If the size of the hidden directory exceeds this percentage, files are purged automatically (starting with the oldest).

7. To specify which drives you want to protect, select **D**rives.

8. Select **O**K.

To turn on Delete Tracker

1. Select **D**elete Protection.

2. Select Delete **T**racker. Select **O**K.

3. Select which drives you want to protect.

4. Select **O**K.

To disable both Delete Sentry and Delete Tracker

1. Select **D**elete Protection.

2. Select **N**one.

3. Select **O**K.

DeskConnect

Beg / Int / Adv   *PCSHELL*

Purpose

Enables you to link a laptop computer to your desktop personal computer and transfer information, data, and files between the laptop and desktop computers.

To run DeskConnect

1. Connect the null-modem cable to the laptop and desktop computers.

2. Type **DESKSRV** at the DOS prompt on the laptop computer.

3. Type **DESKCON** at the DOS prompt on the desktop computer.

4. Run PCSHELL.

5. Press **F10**. From the **S**pecial menu, select Desk**C**onnect.

Command Reference

A dialog box appears, indicating how the laptop's disk drives appear on PC Shell's drive line.

To copy files

1. Select the source drive on the laptop or desktop computer by pressing **Ctrl** plus the drive letter.

   or

   Click the source drive on the laptop or desktop computer (on the drive line).

2. Select the files you want to copy.

3. Select the **F**ile menu by pressing **Alt-F**, then select **C**opy.

   or

   Press **F5**.

   The File Copy dialog box appears.

4. Select the target drive on the laptop or desktop computer by pressing **Ctrl** plus the drive letter. If the target drive has subdirectories, select the subdirectory.

   or

   Click the target drive on the laptop or desktop computer (on the drive line). If the target drive has subdirectories, click the subdirectory.

5. Choose one of the following options:

   Replace **A**ll replaces all files in the target directory that have the same names as the copied files.

   Replace File replaces the file in the target directory that has the same name as the current file.

   Next File skips to the next file of the files you selected to copy (and does not copy the current file).

   Skip All skips all the files you selected to copy and returns to the main PC Shell screen.

   Cancel returns to the main PC Shell screen.

If you try to copy a file into the same subdirectory or onto the same drive, a File Copy dialog box appears. Type a new file name, then select **O**K.

The files are copied to the target location. A File Copy Service dialog box appears while the file(s) are being copied. When copying is complete, you return to the main PC Shell screen.

Desktop

Beg / Int / Adv *DESKTOP*

Purpose

Desktop is a complete desktop organizer that offers nine applications: Notepads, Outlines, Databases, Appointment Scheduler, Modem Telecommunications and Electronic Mail, Macro Editor, Clipboard, Calculators, and Utilities.

To start Desktop at the DOS prompt

1. Type **DESKTOP** at the DOS prompt and press **Enter**.
2. Select **D**esktop.

To run Desktop as memory-resident

Start Desktop at the DOS prompt by typing **DESKTOP /R**.

If your computer has enough memory, Desktop loads into your computer's memory and you run Desktop as a memory-resident program (TSR mode).

To start Desktop when memory-resident

Press **Ctrl-space bar**.

Directory Lock

Beg / Int / Adv *DATAMON*

Purpose

Encrypts and decrypts files as they are written to and read from the specified directories. You can use Directory Lock on a disk or network.

To run Directory Lock

1. From the Data Monitor main menu, select DIrectory Lock.

2. Select Load Directory Lock by pressing **Alt-L**.

3. Use **Tab** to select the Directory Name To Protect text box. Type the names of the directories you want to protect (no backslash is required). For example, to protect the directory C:\WP\REPORTS, type **REPORTS**.

4. To require the user to enter the password periodically, type an amount of time in the Timeout Period text box.

5. To specify the password, select Password by pressing **Alt-P**. Type a password. Select OK to accept the password.

6. To specify the network path (when protecting network directories), select Network by pressing **Alt-N**. Type the path. Do not include the drive letter (which is supplied automatically).

7. After making selections, select OK by pressing **Alt-O**. To stop the operation, select Cancel by pressing **Alt-C**.

Note

To use Directory Lock on a network, run Data Monitor after the network drivers.

Directory Maintenance

Beg / Int / Adv **PCSHELL, DM**

Purpose

Enables you to make a new directory, rename or delete a directory, change to a new directory, prune and graft a subdirectory, and modify attributes of a directory.

To make a new subdirectory

1. Select the drive holding the disk where you want to add the subdirectory. Press **Ctrl-A**, **Ctrl-B**, or **Ctrl-C** to select drive A, B, or C, respectively.

   or

   Click the drive letter on the drive line of the main PC Shell screen.

2. Select the **D**isk menu by pressing **Alt-D**, then select Directory **M**aintenance.

   PC Shell runs the DM program.

3. Select the directory under which you want to make the new subdirectory.

4. Press **F10**. From the **D**irectory menu, select **M**ake Directory.

   or

   Press **F4**.

   or

   From the **D**irectory menu, click **M**ake Directory.

5. Type the name of the new subdirectory (and any extension) in the Make Directory dialog box.

6. Select **O**K to make the new subdirectory.

To rename a directory

1. Select the drive where the directory you want to rename is located. Press **Ctrl-A**, **Ctrl-B**, or **Ctrl-C** to select drive A, B, or C, respectively.

   or

   Click the drive letter on the drive line of the main PC Shell screen.

2. Select the **D**isk menu by pressing **Alt-D**, then select Directory **M**aintenance.

   PC Shell runs the DM program.

3. Select the directory you want to rename.

   You cannot rename the Root Directory on your disk.

4. Press **F10**. From the **D**irectory menu, select **R**ename Directory.

   or

   Press **F5**.

   or

   From the **D**irectory menu, click **R**ename Directory.

5. Type the new name of the directory (and any extension) in the Rename Directory dialog box.

6. Select **O**K to make the new directory.

   If the name you typed in the Rename Directory dialog box is already in use, that name is not accepted.

To delete a directory

1. Select the drive where the directory you want to delete is located. Press **Ctrl-A**, **Ctrl-B**, or **Ctrl-C** to select drive A, B, or C, respectively.

   or

   Click the drive letter on the drive line of the main PC Shell screen.

2. Select the **D**isk menu by pressing **Alt-D**, then select Directory **M**aintenance. PC Shell runs the DM program.

3. Select the directory you want to delete.

   You cannot delete the Root Directory on your disk.

4. Press **F10**. From the **D**irectory menu, select **D**elete Directory.

   or

   Press **F6**.

   or

   From the **D**irectory menu, click **D**elete Directory.

5. Select **O**K to delete the directory. If directory has files you are asked to confirm the deletion.

To prune and graft a subdirectory

1. Select the drive where the subdirectory you want to prune is located. Press **Ctrl-A**, **Ctrl-B**, or **Ctrl-C** to select drive A, B, or C, respectively.

   or

   Click the drive letter on the drive line of the main PC Shell screen.

2. Select the **D**isk menu by pressing **Alt-D**, then select Directory **M**aintenance.

   PC Shell runs the DM program.

3. Select the subdirectory you want to prune.

   You cannot prune the Root Directory on your disk.

4. Press **F10**. From the **D**irectory menu, select Prune & **G**raft.

   or

   Press **F7**.

   or

   From the **D**irectory menu, click Prune & **G**raft.

5. Select the directory where you want to graft the pruned subdirectory. Press **Enter**.

   or

   Double-click the directory where you want to graft the pruned subdirectory.

6. Select **O**K to confirm the graft.

   Pruning and grafting removes the subdirectory (and its files and subdirectories) from its original directory and moves and attaches the subdirectory to the new directory.

To modify directory attributes

1. Select the drive where the subdirectory whose attributes you want to modify is located. Press **Ctrl-A**, **Ctrl-B**, or **Ctrl-C** to select drive A, B, or C, respectively.

   or

Click the drive letter on the drive line of the main PC Shell screen.

2. Select the **D**isk menu by pressing **Alt-D**, then select Directory **M**aintenance.

    PC Shell runs the DM program.

3. Select the directory.

4. Press **F10**. From the **D**irectory menu, select Modify **A**ttributes.

    or

    From the **D**irectory menu, click Modify **A**ttributes.

5. Select **H**idden or **S**ystem to toggle these attributes.

6. Select **O**K to accept the new directory attributes.

Cautions

Although Directory Maintenance is a quick, convenient way to change and move directories, you must be careful. Some programs may require a directory with a specific location or name; if you move or rename that directory, your program may no longer work.

If you use Directory Maintenance to make changes to your directories, you may need to edit your AUTOEXEC.BAT file to update the path statement. You also may need to edit any batch files used to start programs.

If you are using PC Shell as a memory-resident TSR, make certain that no files in the directories you want to change are already in use by another program.

DiskFix

Beg / Int / Adv   *DISKFIX*

Purpose

Scans floppy disks or hard disks for known viruses, damaged data, surface defects, damage to partition tables or boot sectors, cross-linked files, lost cluster chains, and invalid directory entries.

DiskFix can repair damage to partition tables and boot sectors; correct errors such as cross-linked files, lost cluster chains, and invalid directory entries; recover lost cluster chains; recover data from damaged locations and move data to safe locations; and remove surface defects from use.

DiskFix also can perform a nondestructive low-level format on disks. Finally, DiskFix can help to optimize your hard disk's performance by resetting the disk interleave.

To run DiskFix

At the DOS prompt, type **DiskFix** and press **Enter**.

To scan the surface of disk

1. Select **S**urface Scan from the DiskFix main menu.
2. Select the drive you want to scan, then select **O**K.

   DiskFix displays a map of disk tracks with symbols that represent the condition of each cluster and the status of the scan process.

   After identifying damaged data, DiskFix moves the data to safe locations, marking bad locations for future reference.

3. When the scan and repair process is complete, you can generate a report by selecting **O**K. You can send this report to the **P**rinter or to a **F**ile.

To repair a disk

1. Select **R**epair A Disk from the DiskFix main menu.
2. Select the drive you want to repair, then select **O**K.

   DiskFix checks the boot sector, FAT integrity, FAT consistency, media descriptors, FAT validity, directory structure, cross-linked files, and lost clusters, then displays the status of each check.

3. If DiskFix finds an error, an error dialog box appears. Select **R**epair. If DiskFix prompts you for the drive where you want to save information, select a drive, then select **O**K.

   A dialog box displays the status of the repairs.

Command Reference

4. If DiskFix finds lost clusters, you can **S**ave them, **D**elete them, or **I**gnore them. If you decide to save them, they are assigned filenames of the form PCT*nnnnn*.FIX.

5. When repairs are complete, you can generate a report by selecting **O**K. You can send this report to the **P**rinter or to a **F**ile.

To perform a nondestructive low-level format on a disk or set the interleave of a disk

1. Select Re**V**italize A Disk from the DiskFix main menu.

2. Select the drive you want to revitalize, then select **O**K. DiskFix performs a series of tests. After each, select **O**K.

3. If your hard disk cannot undergo a low-level format, DiskFix displays a message. Select **O**K. (Try **S**urface Scan instead.)

4. If your hard disk can undergo a low-level format, the disk is tested for optimum interleave. You then have two options:

   Use The **F**astest Tested Interleave selects the interleave which results in optimum hard drive performance.

   Use The **S**elected Interleave enables you to select any interleave.

5. Select a pattern testing option:

   Read/Write Data–No Pattern Testing reads and writes all data, repairs correctable errors, moves data to safe locations, and does not test further.

   Minimum Pattern Testing is the same as **R**ead/Write Data, but uses 20 test patterns (and takes longer).

   Average Pattern Testing is the same as **R**ead/Write Data, but uses 40 test patterns (and takes much longer).

   Ma**X**imum Pattern Testing is the same as **R**ead/Write Data, but uses 80 test patterns (and takes very much longer).

6. Select **O**K.

To configure DiskFix

1. Select Configure Options from the DiskFix main menu.

2. Select the options you want to use:

    Test Partition Information tests partition and boot sector information of hard disks before displaying the DiskFix main menu.

    Check Boot Sector For Viruses tests the boot sector for viruses before displaying the DiskFix main menu.

    Look For Mirror File searches for Mirror file information which can help to recover data.

    Use Custom Error Messages enables you to customize the messages that the user sees when disk errors are found.

3. Select OK.

To undo a DiskFix repair

1. Select Undo A DiskFix Repair from the DiskFix main menu.

2. Select the drive on which you saved the original disk information.

    To restore the disk, you must have saved the information when prompted in Repair A Disk.

3. Select OK.

Caution

Turn off disk caches (other than PC-Cache) before using DiskFix.

Note

DiskFix is more likely to fix your disk if you use Mirror regularly. See *Mirror* for details.

Command Reference

Disk Information

Adv *PCSHELL*

Purpose

Provides information about a disk's volume label, total disk space, available disk space, number and total size of hidden files, number and total size of user files, number and total size of directories, number of bytes located in a bad sector, bytes per sector, sectors per cluster, sectors per track, total clusters, total sectors, total tracks, number of sides, and number of cylinders.

To obtain disk information

1. Select the disk about which you want information. Press **Ctrl-A**, **Ctrl-B**, or **Ctrl-C** to select drive A, B, or C, respectively.

   or

   Click the drive letter on the drive line of the main PC Shell screen.

2. Select the **D**isk menu by pressing **Alt-D**, then select Disk **I**nformation.

3. After reviewing the Disk Information dialog box, select **O**K to return to the main PC Shell screen.

Disk Light

Beg / Int / Adv *DATAMON*

Purpose

Indicates when floppy disks or hard disks are being accessed by displaying the drive letter and type of access in the upper right corner of the screen.

To use Disk Light

1. Type **DATAMON** at the DOS prompt.

2. From the Data Monitor main menu, select Disk **L**ight.

3. Select **L**oad Disk Light, then select **O**K.

To activate Disk Light when you boot your computer

Add the following line to your computer's AUTOEXEC.BAT file:

DATAMON /LIGHT+

Notes

Disk Light is disabled in Windows.

To use Disk Light on a network, run Data Monitor after the network drivers.

Disk Map

Adv *PCSHELL*

Purpose

Displays the disk sectors or clusters in use and the sectors that are free or available for use.

Disk Map symbols

In the Disk Mapping dialog box, each position on the grid represents one cluster (except when displaying large hard disks, where each position represents 1/1000th of the total space). DOS allocates space for a file in clusters. Clusters can be different sizes, however, depending on the disk you use. Each position displays one of the following symbols:

[ ]	Available	Cluster is not used; available for file storage.
[B]	Boot record	Cluster contains the disk's boot record.
[F]	File Alloc Table	Cluster contains the File Allocation Table (FAT).
[D]	Directory	Cluster contains the disk's directory.
[·]	Allocated	Cluster is part of a file.

Command Reference

[H]	Hidden	Cluster is part of a hidden file.
[R]	Read Only	Cluster is part of a read-only file.
[X]	Bad Cluster	DOS has marked this cluster as bad and has made it unusable.

To map a disk

1. Select the disk you want to map. Press **Ctrl-A**, **Ctrl-B**, or **Ctrl-C** to select drive A, B, or C, respectively.

   or

   Click the drive letter on the drive line of the main PC Shell screen.

2. Select the **S**pecial menu by pressing **Alt-S**, then select Disk **M**ap.

3. To return to the main PC Shell screen, select **C**ancel.

Edit File

Int / Adv   *PCSHELL*

Purpose

Enables you to create or edit a text file.

To edit a file

1. Select the file you want to edit.

2. Select the **F**ile menu by pressing **Alt-F**, then select Chan**G**e File.

3. Select **E**dit File, then select **O**K.

   PC Shell runs the DESKTOP function. The file appears on-screen.

4. Edit the file. For editing information, see *Notepads*.

5. To save your changes, select the **F**ile menu by pressing **Alt-F**, then select **S**ave. Then select **S**ave again by pressing **Alt-S**.

   To exit without saving, select the **F**ile menu by pressing **Alt-F**, then select E**X**it Without Saving.

6. To exit after saving, press **Esc**.

Caution

Do not edit files with COM or EXE extensions (to do so can cause problems in running your programs).

Exit PC Shell

Beg / Int / Adv *PCSHELL*

Purpose

Enables you to exit the PC Shell program and return to the DOS prompt.

To exit PC Shell

1. Select the **F**ile menu by pressing **Alt-F**, then select E**X**it.

   or

   Press **F3**.

2. To confirm that you want to exit, select **O**K.

Fax Telecommunications

Beg / Int / Adv *DESKTOP*

Purpose

Enables you to send and receive faxes through your computer. (Your computer must have a fax board.)

Command Reference

To start Fax Telecommunications

1. From the main **D**esktop menu, select **T**elecommunications, then select **S**end A Fax.

   The display shows current fax destination entries, including their entry numbers, the name and fax number where the fax will be sent, and the fax type.

2. The following function keys are available:

   F4 Adds a new entry.

   F5 Edits the selected entry.

   F6 Deletes the selected entry.

   F7 Sends files to the selected entry.

   F8 Displays the Fax Log.

To configure Fax Telecommunications

1. Select the **C**onfigure menu.

2. Select configuration options:

   Fax Drive specifies the directory to store the fax files. Type the new directory name, press **Enter**, then select **O**K by pressing **Alt-O**.

   Page Length sets the page size of the destination machine. Type the new page length, press **Enter**, then select **O**K.

   Cover Page specifies whether to send the cover page. Press **Enter** to toggle this feature, then select **O**K.

   Time Format specifies AM/PM or 24-hour time format. Select **O**K.

   Sent From tells Fax Telecommunications who is sending the fax. Type your name, press **Enter**, then select **O**K by pressing **Alt-O**.

To send a fax to a new destination

1. From the **A**ctions menu, select **A**dd A New Entry.

2. Type the following information. Press **Tab** to move between text boxes.

Date	The date to send the fax.
Time	The time to send the fax.
From	Changes the preset configuration Sent From option.
To	The destination of the fax.
Fax Number	The destination fax number.
Comments	Optional comments for your use.

3. Select from the following options:

Normal Resolution	Use for most faxes, but not for graphics. (Faster)
Fine Resolution	Use for especially sharp faxes or for graphics. (Slower)
Fax Board to Fax Board	Use to send binary files.

4. To send an existing file, select **S**elect Files And Send by pressing **Alt-S**. Select the file you want to send, then select **A**dd by pressing **Alt-A**. Select **S**end by pressing **Alt-S**.

   To create and send a new file, select **M**ake A New File And Send by pressing **Alt-M**. Type the name of the new file, then select **O**K. Type the contents of the file, then press **Esc**.

5. If you want to send a cover page, select **O**K. Type the cover page, then press **Esc**.

6. Select **O**K.

To send a fax to an existing destination

1. Select the destination for the fax you want to send.

2. From the **A**ctions menu, select **S**end Files To Selected Entry.

3. Select **S**elect Files And Send.

Command Reference

4. To send any files you sent previously, select **S**end.

   To send other files, select **C**hoose Different Files. Select the files you want to send and select **A**dd for each file. Then select **S**end.

5. If you want to send a cover page, select **O**K. Type the cover page, then press **Esc**.

6. Select **O**K.

To edit a fax destination entry

1. Select the destination entry you want to edit.

2. From the **A**ctions menu, select **E**dit The Current Entry.

3. Type the information you want to change.

4. Select **S**elect Files And Send or select **M**ake A New File and follow the steps for sending a new fax.

To delete a fax entry

1. Select the entry you want to delete.

2. From the **A**ctions menu, select **D**elete The Current Entry.

FileFind

Beg / Int / Adv   *FF*

Purpose

Searches for files; finds duplicate files; compares and views retrieved files; deletes, renames, copies, or changes attributes of files. The files can be on disks or on networks.

To start FileFind

Type **FF** at the DOS prompt, then press **Enter**.

To find a file

1. To specify file names, select File S**P**ecification by pressing **Alt-P**, then enter the file specifications. You can use the DOS wildcard characters * and ? and the exclude character – (the minus sign).

2. To look for text contained in files, select **C**ontaining by pressing **Alt-C**. Enter the text you want to find.

   The following options are also available:

   Ignore Case (**Alt-I**) selects whether the search is case-sensitive.

   Whole Word (**Alt-W**) selects whether to find parts of words or to find entire words only.

3. To select the drive or directory to search, select D**R**ives by pressing **Alt-R**.

   or

   Select the **S**earch menu by pressing **Alt-S**, then select **S**elected Drives.

   Select drives using the arrow keys. To toggle a drive on or off, press **Enter**.

   Change the selected directory by pressing **Alt-D**.

   Select from the following options for drive and directory searches:

   Entire Drive (**Alt-E**) searches the entire drive.

   Current Directory And **B**elow (**Alt-B**) searches within the current directory and its subdirectories.

   Curren**T** Directory Only (**Alt-T**) searches only within the current directory.

   After selecting drive and directory options, select **O**K to continue.

4. To filter files by attributes, date, time or size select Fi**L**ters.

   or

   Select the **S**earch menu by pressing **Alt-S**, then select Fi**L**ters.

Select from the following attribute filter options:

REad Only
System
Hidden
Archive
Only These AttribUtes
IncludinG These Attributes

For a date and time filter, select Modified After/Before by pressing **Tab**.

For a size filter, select SiZe Greater/Less by pressing **Tab**.

After selecting filter options, select **O**K to continue.

5. To start the search, press **Enter**.

   or

   Select STart by pressing **Alt-T**.

6. You can view, copy, rename, delete, move, or change the attributes of any matching file. Select the File menu by pressing **Alt-F**, then select the appropriate command.

7. You can sort any matching files for display with various pieces of information. Select the Display menu by pressing **Alt-D**, then select the display format and sorting criteria.

To find duplicate files

1. From the Search menu, select Find Duplicates.

2. To select the drive or directory to search, select DRives by pressing **Alt-R**.

   or

   Select the Search menu by pressing **Alt-S**, then select Selected Drives.

   Select drives using the arrow keys. To toggle each drive on or off, press **Enter**.

   Change the selected directory by pressing **Alt-D**.

Select from the following options for drive and directory searches:

Entire Drive (**Alt-E**) searches the entire drive.

Current Directory And **B**elow (**Alt-B**) searches within the current directory and its subdirectories.

Curren**T** Directory Only (**Alt-T**) searches only within the current directory.

After selecting drive and directory options, select **O**K to continue.

3. To filter files by name, size, or date, select Fi**L**ters.

   or

   Select the **S**earch menu by pressing **Alt-S**, then select Fi**L**ters.

   Select from the following attribute filter options:

   Name
   Name, **S**ize
   Name, Size, **D**ate

   After selecting filter options, select **O**K to continue.

4. To start the search, press **Enter**.

   or

   Select S**T**art by pressing **Alt-T**.

To select from the retrieved files

1. To select files one-by-one, move the cursor to the file and press **Enter**.

2. To select all files, select the **F**ile menu by pressing **Alt-F**, then select **S**elect All Files.

To sort the retrieved files

1. Select the **D**isplay menu by pressing **Alt-D**, then select **S**ort By.

2. Select the sort criterion:

   Unsorted   Displays files in the order of the directory.

Command Reference

Name	Sorts by file name.
Si**Z**e	Sorts by file size.
E**X**tension	Sorts by extension.
Da**T**e and Time	Sorts by date and time.

On a network, additional sorting criteria are available.

3. Select Ascending or Descending sort order.
4. Select **O**K by pressing **Alt-O**.

To change file display options

1. Select the **D**isplay menu by pressing **Alt-D**, the select **L**ist Format.
2. Select the information you want to display:

Size	The file size in bytes.
Attributes	The file attributes.
Modified Date	The date the file was last modified.
Modified **T**ime	The time the file was last modified.

On a network, additional information is available.

3. Select **O**K by pressing **Alt-O**.

To view, copy, rename, delete, move, or change attributes of files

1. Select files from the Matching Files list.
2. Select the **F**ile menu by pressing **Alt-F**.
3. Select **V**iew, **C**opy, R**E**name, **D**elete, or Set **A**ttributes.

FileFix

Beg / Int / Adv **FILEFIX**

Purpose

Recovers damaged Lotus 1-2-3, Lotus Symphony, and dBASE files. In Lotus 1-2-3 and Symphony files, FileFix can repair invalid cell entries; invalid version number; and damaged format, global setting, and formula cells. In dBASE files, FileFix can repair damaged file headers, zapped files, record frame error, embedded end-of-file characters, and other illegal characters.

To start FileFix

Type **FILEFIX** at the DOS prompt, then press **Enter**.

To fix a Lotus 1-2-3 file

1. Select **L**otus 1-2-3 from the FileFix main menu.

2. Select the file you want to repair. Select **O**K.

3. Select repair options:

    Recover **A**ll Data attempts to recover the entire file. (Suggested)

    Recover Cell **D**ata Only attempts to recover cell data only, without formatting information. Use this option if Recover **A**ll Data fails.

4. If the file has a password, select File Is **P**assword Protected. Type the password. Select **O**K.

5. Select **O**K.

To fix a Symphony file

1. Select **S**ymphony from the FileFix main menu.

2. Select the file you want to repair. Select **O**K.

3. Select repair options:

    Recover **A**ll Data attempts to recover the entire file. (Suggested)

    Recover Cell **D**ata Only attempts to recover cell data only, without formatting information. Use this option if Recover **A**ll Data fails.

4. If the file has a password, select File Is **P**assword Protected. Type the password. Select **O**K.

5. Select **O**K.

To fix a dBASE file

1. Select **D**BASE from the FileFix main menu.

2. Select the file you want to repair. Select **O**K.

3. Select the repair method:

   Automatic **R**ecovery attempts to repair the file without any assistance. (Easiest)

   Display **D**amaged Records Before Fixing enables you to evaluate each damaged record. (Next easiest)

   Display **E**ach record enables you to evaluate every record. (Least easy)

4. Select repair options:

   Check Data **A**lignment checks data alignment as the file is repaired.

   Check for **B**inary And Graphics Characters replaces these characters with spaces. Select this option unless you want the file to contain graphics characters.

   File Was Created With Clipper uses Clipper field limits.

5. Select **O**K.

File Map

Adv   *PCSHELL*

Purpose

Displays the sectors and clusters used by the selected file. With this map, you can determine whether your files are fragmented (whether the file's sectors are scattered throughout the disk). If your files are fragmented, you do not obtain maximum performance from your computer's disk drive.

File Map symbols

The File Map uses the same symbols as the Disk Map. For more information, see *Disk Map*.

To map a file

1. Select the file(s) you want to map.

   If you do not select any files, PC Shell displays a map for each file in the selected subdirectory.

2. Select the **S**pecial menu by pressing **Alt-S**, then select **F**ile Map.

3. Select **N**ext to see a map of the next selected file (or, if you did not select any files, the next file in the selected subdirectory). Select **P**rior to see a map of the preceding selected file (or, if you did not select any files, the preceding file in the subdirectory).

4. To return to the main PC Shell screen, select **C**ancel.

Format Data Disk

Beg / Int / Adv   ***PCSHELL, PCFORMAT***

Purpose

Initializes every track on the disk so that your computer recognizes the disk and uses it to store your data files.

To format a data disk

1. Insert a blank disk into drive A or B.

2. Select the **D**isk menu by pressing **Alt-D**, then select **F**ormat Data Disk.

   PC Shell runs the PCFORMAT program.

3. In the Drive Selection dialog box, select the drive holding the blank disk. Select **O**K to continue.

4. Select format options from the Select Format Options dialog box.

   Depending on your computer, one or more of the following disk options are available:

160K — Single-sided floppy disk, 8 sectors per track, 40 tracks.

180K — Single-sided floppy disk, 9 sectors per track, 40 tracks.

320K — Double-sided floppy disk, 8 sectors per track, 40 tracks.

360K — Double-sided floppy disk, 9 sectors per track, 40 tracks.

1.2M — High-density floppy disk, double-sided, 15 sectors per track, 80 tracks.

720K — 3 1/2-inch diskette, double-sided, 9 sectors per track, 80 tracks.

1.44M — High-density 3 1/2-inch diskette, double-sided, 18 sectors per track, 80 tracks.

Depending on the computer and version of DOS you use, you may need to install the DOS DRIVER.SYS in your CONFIG.SYS file before all formatting options are available in the Select Format Options dialog box.

The following types of format are available:

Safe Format — Formats disk so it can be recovered using Unformat.

Quick Format — Quickly reformats previously formatted disk, including RAM disk or Bernoulli box.

Full Format — Similar to Safe Format, but can repair marginal sectors. Not available for hard disk.

Destructive **F**ormat	Formats disk and erases all data. The disk cannot be recovered with Unformat. Not available for the hard disk.

The following additional options are available:

Install System Files	Installs system files on disk after formatting. You can then use the disk to start (boot) the computer.
Save **M**irror Info	Runs the Mirror program for this disk. Mirror can help to recover files later.
Label	Enables you to create an optional label for the disk.

5. After selecting options, select **O**K to proceed with the formatting of your disk. The Formatting dialog box displays the status.

6. To return to the main PC Shell menu, select **O**K, then **C**ancel, then E**X**it (**Alt-X**), then **O**K.

Caution

This command may destroy all files or data already stored on your disk. Unlike the DOS FORMAT command, disks formatted with this command may not be recoverable.

Help

Beg / Int / Adv   *PCSHELL*

Purpose

Assists in locating commands and provides descriptions of what the commands do.

Command Reference

To get help

1. Select **H**elp by pressing **Alt-H**.

   or

   Press **F1** for context-sensitive Help screens.

2. To display topics (Help chapter headings), select **T**opics. Move the selection bar to the topic you want to see and press **Enter**.

   or

   Press **F4**.

3. To display an index (with keywords), select **I**ndex. Move the selection bar to the keyword you want to use and press **Enter**.

   or

   Press **F2**.

4. To scroll through help information on-screen, use the cursor keys.

Hex Edit File

Int / Adv   *PCSHELL*

Purpose

Enables you to view and edit a file as ASCII text or hexadecimal values.

To view and edit a file

1. Select the file(s) you want to edit.

2. Select the **F**ile menu by pressing **Alt-F**, then select Chan**G**e File.

3. Select **H**ex Edit File.

4. To toggle between formatted text mode (ASCII) and Hex mode (primarily used for editing), press **F5**. You cannot edit or change a file while in formatted text mode.

5. To change to a different relative sector within the selected file, press **F6** to select Change Sector, then enter the new sector number, then select **O**K by pressing **Alt-O**.

6. To move to the next selected file, press **F9**.

7. To edit the file, press **F7**.

   The following key commands are available during editing:

Key	Action
F8	Toggles between editing ASCII text and hexadecimal values.
F5	Saves changes to disk.
Home	Moves to the beginning of the file.
End	Moves to the end of the file.
PgUp	Moves back one screen.
PgDn	Moves forward one screen.
Esc	Ends editing without saving.

   You also can use the scroll bars on the right side of the screen (with the mouse) to scroll through the file.

8. To exit and return to the main PC Shell screen, press **F3**.

To repair a bad sector in a file

1. Select the **F**ile menu by pressing **Alt-F**, then select Chan**G**e File.

2. Select **H**ex Edit File.

3. To change to the bad relative sector within the selected file, press **F6** to select Change Sector. Enter the new sector number, then select **O**K by pressing **Alt-O**.

4. To edit the file, press **F7**.

5. Edit the bad sector.

Command Reference

6. Save the sector by pressing **F5** to rewrite the same sector information—without the error—onto your disk.

   This procedure should make the sector readable, but some information rewritten on the sector may be invalid. This procedure recovers as much of the data as possible.

Caution

Before using this command, you need a good working knowledge of ASCII and hexadecimal values and an understanding of sector bytes. Making improper changes to files with the **H**ex Edit File command can make programs inoperable.

Hide All Lists

Beg / Int / Adv   *PCSHELL*

Purpose

Enables you to hide all lists in order to see the underlying screen.

To hide all lists

Select the **V**iew menu by pressing **Alt-V**, then select **H**ide All Lists.

Keyboard Macros

Beg / Int / Adv   *DESKTOP*

Purpose

Enables you to record a series of keystrokes, then repeat them by pressing a simple key combination.

To open the Macro Editor

1. Select **M**acro Editor from the main **D**esktop menu.

2. Select a file in the Macro Files dialog box.

3. Select **L**oad by pressing **Alt-L**.

To write a macro

To record certain keystrokes, you must press **F7** before you press that key. For example, to record **Backspace** as one of the keystrokes in a macro (rather than to use the **Backspace** key to edit the file) you must press **F7**, then press **Backspace**. The **F7** means "insert into the macro the next key pressed."

1. Select **M**acro Editor from the main **D**esktop menu.

2. Select **N**ew by pressing **Alt-N**.

3. Type the new macro. The following is an example of a macro created in the Macro Editor:

    <begdef><ctrlp>Que Books<enddef>

    This macro defines the **Ctrl-P** combination to type the words "Que Books."

4. To save the macro, select **F**ile by pressing **Alt-F**, then select **S**ave.

    or

    Press **F5**.

5. Type a file name for the macro, using the PRO extension. Press **Enter**.

6. Select **O**K.

To set macro activation options

1. Press **F10**. From the **F**ile menu, select **M**acro Activation.

    or

    Press **F8**.

2. Use the arrow keys to select one of the following options:

Not Active	No files play back.
Active When In PC Tools Desktop	Macros in the current file play back only when you are in PC Tools Desktop.

Command Reference

Active When Not In PC Tools Desktop	Macros in the current file play back everywhere *except* when you are in PC Tools Desktop.
Active Everywhere	Macros in the current file play back everywhere.

3. Select **O**K to accept macro activation options or **C**ancel to ignore changes.

To use Learn Mode

PC Tools Desktop must be memory-resident to use Learn Mode.

1. Press **F10**. From the **C**ontrols menu, select **L**earn Mode. A check mark appears next to Learn Mode in the **C**ontrols menu.

2. Press **Ctrl-space bar** to leave Desktop.

3. When you are ready for the Macro Editor to record your keystrokes, press **Alt-+** (the "+" at the top of the keyboard).

   The cursor changes shape to indicate that the Macro Editor is recording.

4. Press the keystroke combination you want to use for this macro, such as **Ctrl-G**.

5. Type the commands and keystrokes you want to record.

6. After you type the commands and keystrokes, press **Alt--**(the "-" at the top of the keyboard).

   The cursor changes back to its original shape.

7. Return to the Macro Editor (by pressing **Ctrl-space bar**, then selecting **D**esktop, then selecting **M**acro Editor) and turn off Learn Mode (by selecting the **C**ontrols menu, then **L**earn Mode).

   Learn Mode is active until you return to the Macro Editor and turn it off. Learn Mode creates a file called LEARN.PRO, which you can rename and edit. You also can paste the macros into separate files.

To edit text in the Macro Editor

The commands to edit text in the Macro Editor are similar to the commands used in the Clipboard and Notepads.

To save the macro setup

Press **F10**. From the **C**ontrols menu, select **S**ave Setup.

Notes

You can use the Macro Editor in other programs if PC Tools Desktop is memory-resident. If PC Tools Desktop is not resident in your computer's memory, the macros work only in Desktop.

To prevent accidental erasure or loss of data, some programs (such as PC Secure, CP Backup, and Compress) cannot be started with a macro.

Locate File

Beg / Int / Adv *PCSHELL, FF*

Purpose

Enables you to locate a file (or text contained in a file) anywhere on a disk.

To locate a file

1. Select the **F**ile menu by pressing **Alt-F**, then select **L**ocate File.

   or

   Press **F7**.

   PC Shell runs the FF function.

2. To search for file names, select File S**P**ecification by pressing **Alt-P**. Enter one or more file specifications, using the DOS wildcard characters * and ? and exclude character – (minus sign).

3. To search for text contained in files, select **C**ontaining by pressing **Alt-C**. (You cannot search for text when searching for duplicate files.)

Command Reference

Enter the text you want to find.

Select from the following options for text searches:

Ignore Case (**Alt-I**) selects whether the search is case-sensitive.

Whole Word (**Alt-W**) selects whether to find parts of words or to find entire words only.

4. To select the drive or directory to search, select D**R**ives by pressing **Alt-R**.

   or

   Select the **S**earch menu by pressing **Alt-S**, then select **S**elected Drives.

   Select the drive(s) by using the arrow keys. To toggle a drive on or off, press **Enter**.

   Change the selected directory by pressing **Alt-D**.

   Select from the following options for drive and directory searches:

   Entire Drive (**Alt-E**) searches the entire drive.

   Current Directory And **B**elow (**Alt-B**) searches within the current directory and its subdirectories.

   Curren**T** Directory Only (**Alt-T**) searches only within the current directory.

   After selecting drive and directory options, select **O**K to continue.

5. To filter files by attributes, date, time, or size, select Fi**L**ters.

   or

   Select the **S**earch menu by pressing **Alt-S**, then select Fi**L**ters.

   Select from the following options for attribute filters:

   R**E**ad Only
   System
   Hidden
   Archive
   Only These Attrib**U**tes

IncludinG These Attributes

For a date and time filter, select Modified After/Before by pressing Tab.

For a size filter, select SiZe Greater/Less by pressing Tab.

After selecting filter options, select OK to continue.

6. To start the search, press Enter.

   or

   Select STart by pressing Alt-T.

7. To view, copy, rename, delete, move, or change the attributes of any matching files, select the File menu by pressing Alt-F, then select the appropriate command.

8. To sort any matching files for display with various items of information, select the Display menu by pressing Alt-D, then select the display format and sorting criteria.

9. To return to PC Shell select OK; otherwise, select Cancel.

   PC Shell displays all matching files in the Located Files list. You can apply all the usual PC Shell commands to these files.

10. To leave the list, press Esc.

Make Disk Bootable

Beg / Int / Adv **PCSHELL, PCFORMAT**

Purpose

Transfers the DOS system files to a previously formatted disk so that you can use that disk to start (boot) your computer.

To make a system disk

1. Insert a blank formatted disk into drive A or B.

2. Select the **D**isk menu by pressing **Alt-D**, then select Make Disk **B**ootable.

   PC Shell runs the PCFORMAT function.

3. Select the drive from the Drive Selection dialog box.

4. Select **O**K to continue.

5. Select the format size for the disk, then select **OK**.

6. A message appears telling you that the format is completed. To return to PC Shell, select **OK**, then **Alt-X**.

Note

When you create a system disk, that disk must not contain any files (because the system files must have a specific location on the disk). If any problem occurs, PC Shell reports the error during execution of the command.

Memory Information

Beg / Int / Adv *MI*

Purpose

Displays a summary of your computer's memory information, including conventional memory installed and available, extended and expanded memory available, and the amount of space each TSR uses.

To run MI

Type **MI** at the DOS prompt, then press **Enter**.

Memory Map

Adv *PCSHELL, SI*

Purpose

Displays the type, location, and size of DOS memory blocks; the names of the applications using the blocks; and any vectors used.

To run Memory Map

1. Select the **S**pecial menu by pressing **Alt-S**, then select M**E**mory Map.

   PC Shell runs the SI function.

2. Select **L**ist.

   The Conventional Memory List appears. Use the **up arrow** and **down arrow** to select programs in memory and to display their command line parameters, vectors used, and memory blocks used.

3. For more information, select D**E**tails.

4. For a summary of memory blocks, select St**A**tistics.

5. To return to the main PC Shell screen, select **O**K from the main Memory Map menu.

Mirror

Beg / Int / Adv   *MIRROR*

Purpose

Keeps a copy of the File Allocation Table (FAT) and root directory of your hard disk in a hidden file.

To run Mirror

Type **MIRROR** at the DOS prompt, then press **Enter**.

To install Delete Tracker

Type **MIRROR /T***d* at the DOS prompt, then press **Enter**. The letter *d* represents the drive you want to protect with Delete Tracker.

Notes

Mirror saves information that can help you to recover if you accidentally damage the files on your disk by running DOS ERASE, RECOVER, or FORMAT. Use Unformat with the Mirror data to recover the disk if you experience a major loss of data from using these DOS commands.

Command Reference 81

Unformat can recover only those files reported in MIRROR. To ensure that you can recover all files, run Mirror on a regular schedule.

Modify Display

Beg / Int / Adv   *PCSHELL*

Purpose

Establishes the way PC Shell displays files and lists.

To switch between Tree List, File List, and drive line windows

Press **Tab** to switch between windows.

or

Click the mouse button in the window you want to activate.

To switch to the Dual File Lists display

1. Press **Ins**.

   or

   Select the **V**iew menu by pressing **Alt-V**, then select **D**ual File Lists.

2. Select a second directory or drive in either Tree List window.

To switch to the Single File List display

Press **Del**.

or

Select the **V**iew menu by pressing **Alt-V**, then select **S**ingle File List.

To select the File List filter or File Select filter

1. Select the directory holding the files you want to display.

2. Select the **V**iew menu by pressing **Alt-V**, then select Fi**L**ters.

3. Select File **L**ist or File **S**elect.

4. Type the file name and the extension you want to display.

5. To accept the File List filter, select **D**isplay by pressing **Alt-D**.

   or

   To select the files specified by the File Select filter, select **S**elect by pressing **Alt-S**.

   To reset the file name and extension, select **R**eset by pressing **Alt-R** (while in the File List Filter dialog box).

   To abandon the File List Filter or File Select Filter dialog box, select **C**ancel by pressing **Alt-C**.

6. After using the File **L**ist command to list a group of files, you must issue the command again to list all files. (To display all files in the File List window, select **R**eset in the File List Filter dialog box.)

To change the file display options

1. Select the **O**ptions menu by pressing **Alt-O**, then select **F**ile Display Options.

   or

   Press **F6**.

2. Select any of the Display Options or the File Sort Options in the Display Options dialog box.

   You can display files with the following options:

Size	Displays the file's size.
Date	Displays the date the file was last modified.
Time	Displays the time the file was last modified.
Attribute	Displays the file's attributes.
Number Of C**L**usters	Displays the number of clusters in the file.

Command Reference

You can sort files according to the following options:

NaMe — Sorts files according to file name.

EXt — Sorts files according to extension.

SiZe — Sorts files according to size.

DatE/Time — Sorts files according to date and time.

None — Does not sort the files. Lists the files in the order they appear in the directory.

AscendIng — Sorts files according to the selected option, in ascending order.

DescendinG — Sorts files according to the selected option, in descending order.

3. Select **OK** to change the File Display options and to return to the main PC Shell menu.

To unselect files

Select the **V**iew menu by pressing **Alt-V**, then select **U**nselect Files.

or

Move the highlight bar to the selected file and press **Enter**.

or

Press **F4**.

or

Click the selected file with the left mouse button.

To save a configuration

Select the **O**ptions menu by pressing **Alt-O**, then select S**A**ve Configuration File.

Modify Program List

Int / Adv   *PCSHELL*

Purpose

Enables you to change the list of programs displayed in the PC Shell Program List. You can add, delete, or edit the applications displayed in the menu.

To add a new program to the Program List

1. Press **F10**.

   The Program List appears.

2. Press **F4**, select **I**tem, then select **OK**.

3. Enter information about the new program. To move between fields, press **Tab**. Available fields include the following:

Program Title	The name to appear in the Program List.
Commands	DOS commands or application programs, such as WP.EXE.
Startup Directory	The application's expected directory.
Password	The (optional) password to run the application.

4. To create a text file describing this program (which you can view by pressing **F2** when you select that program in the Program List), do the following:

   Select **D**escription by pressing **Alt-D**.

   Type the description.

   Select the **F**ile menu by pressing **Alt-F**, then select **S**ave.

   Enter a file name, then select **S**ave by pressing **Alt-S**.

   Press **F3** or **Esc** to exit.

Command Reference 85

5. After selecting options, select **OK**.
6. To return to PC Shell menu, press **F10**.

To modify the Program List

1. Select the program you want to modify.
2. Select Edit (**F5**), Delete (**F6**), Cut (**F7**), Copy (**F8**), or Paste (**F9**).
3. If you are adding or editing, type the information about your application program in the dialog box. Press **Tab** to move between entries.
4. Press **F10** to return to the main PC Shell menu.

Move File

Beg / Int / Adv   *PCSHELL*

Purpose

Enables you to move one or many files to another directory on the same drive or to another drive.

To move files

1. Select the file(s) you want to move.
2. Select the **F**ile menu by pressing **Alt-F**, then select **M**ove File.

   A message box warns you that the command will delete the source file(s).
3. Confirm the move by selecting **OK** in the message box.
4. If you are using the Dual Files List display, PC Shell asks whether the other window is the window to which you want to move the files. To move the files to that window, select **OK**; otherwise, select **N**o.
5. Select the target drive in the File Move box using the arrow keys. Press **Enter**, then select **OK**.
6. Select the directory to which you want to move the file(s). If the target directory contains files with the

same file names, select one of the following options:

Replace **A**ll replaces all files in the target directory with the moved files having the same names.

Replace File replaces the current file in the target with the moved file having the same name.

Skip **F**ile skips to the next selected file. The current file is not moved.

Skip All skips all the selected files and returns to the main PC Shell screen.

Cancel returns to the main PC Shell screen.

If the target directory is the same as the source directory, the Move dialog box displays the following message:

```
Cannot move file to same path.
```

Select **C**ancel.

Otherwise, the files are moved to the new location and you return to the main PC Shell screen.

Network Info

Beg / Int / Adv *PCSHELL, SI*

Purpose

Checks and reports extensive information on network and user status and enables you to send messages to users.

To display general network information

1. Select the **S**pecial menu by pressing **Alt-S**, then select **S**ystem Info.

   PC Shell runs the SI function.

2. Select Ne**T**work.

   PC Shell displays servers, number of users, current user, login time and date, and connection number.

3. Continue with any of the following sets of steps.

Command Reference

To display information about network users

Display network information, then select **U**ser List.

PC Shell displays users logged on, login times and dates, and connection numbers.

To send a message to selected users

1. Display network information, then select **U**ser List.
2. Select users from the list using the arrow keys, then select Se**L**ect User.
3. Select M**E**ssage.
4. Type the message. Press **Enter**.
5. Select Send M**E**ssage.

To see disk space used by selected users

1. Display network information, then select **U**ser List.
2. Select users from the list using the arrow keys, then select Se**L**ect User.
3. Select D**I**sk Space.

To display network group information

1. Display network information, then select **G**roup List.

   PC Shell displays the Group List for the selected server.

2. To see the list of users logged on, select users from the list using the arrow keys, then select O**N**line Members.

3. To see the list of users for the selected group, select M**E**mber List.

To display network detail information

Display network information, then select D**E**tails.

PC Shell displays the network name, version, serial number, number of connections supported and used, number of volumes supported, SFT level, TTS level, etc.

Notepads

Beg / Int / Adv *DESKTOP*

Purpose
Performs simple word processing (including editing, cutting and pasting, searching and replacing, printing, and checking spelling), and can send files as electronic mail.

To start Notepads
From main **D**esktop menu, select **N**otepads.

To create a new Notepads file
Select **N**ew by pressing **Alt-N**.

To load an existing Notepads file
1. Press **F10**. From the **F**ile menu, select **L**oad.
2. Type the file name. You can include the DOS wildcard characters **?** and *****. Press **Enter**.
3. If more than one file matches the file name you typed, select the file from the list in the Load Form dialog box.
4. To load the form, select **L**oad by pressing **Alt-L**.

To save a Notepads file
1. Press **F10**. From the **F**ile menu, select **S**ave.
2. Type the file name. Press **Enter**.
3. Press **Tab** to select any of the following options:

PC Tools Desktop	Saves the file in a PC Tools Desktop file format.
ASCII	Saves the file as a regular ASCII file.
Make Backup File	Creates a second (backup) file with the same file name, but with the extension BAK.

4. To save the file, select **S**ave by pressing **Alt-S**.

To exit from Notepads without saving

Press F10. From the File menu, select EXit Without Saving.

To use Autosave in Notepads

1. Press F10. From the File menu, select Autosave.

2. Type the number of minutes you want to elapse between autosaves.

3. Press Tab to turn on the automatic save feature.

4. To accept the automatic save setup, select OK by pressing Alt-O.

To print a Notepads file

1. Press F10. From the File menu, select Print.

2. Press Tab to select any of the following options:

Device	LPT1, LPT2, LPT3, COM1, COM2, or Disk File.
Number Of Copies	Type the number of copies you want to print, then press Enter.
Line Spacing	Type the number for line spacing, then press Enter.
Starting Page Number	Type the page number of the first page you want to print, then press Enter.

3. To start printing, select Print by pressing Alt-P.

To send a Notepads file as electronic mail

Press F10. From the File menu, select Send Electronic Mail.

To edit text in Notepads

Use the keyboard editing commands or use the mouse to position the cursor.

The following keyboard commands are available:

Key	Action
Any character	Inserts the character at the cursor.
space bar	Inserts a space at the cursor.
Tab	Inserts a tab at the cursor.
Enter	Inserts a paragraph break at the cursor.
Del	Deletes the character at the cursor.
Ins	Toggles between Insert and Overwrite modes.
Backspace	Deletes the character to the left of the cursor.
up arrow	Moves the cursor up one line.
down arrow	Moves the cursor down one line.
left arrow	Moves the cursor left one character.
right arrow	Moves the cursor right one character.
Ctrl-left arrow	Moves to the beginning of the next word.
Ctrl-right arrow	Moves to the end of the preceding word.
Home	Moves to the beginning of the line.
End	Moves to the end of the line.
Ctrl-Home	Moves to the beginning of the file.
Ctrl-End	Moves to the end of the file.

Key	Action
Home Home	Moves to the beginning of the window.
End End	Moves to the end of the window.
PgUp	Scrolls text up one window.
PgDn	Scrolls text down one window.

To mark a block of text

1. Move the cursor to where you want to begin marking text.

2. Press **F10**. From the **E**dit menu, select **M**ark Block.

3. Move the cursor to where you want to end the marked text.

To unmark a block of text

Press **F10**. From the **E**dit menu, select **U**nmark Block.

To copy text to the Clipboard

1. Move the cursor to where you want to start copying text into the Clipboard.

2. Press **F10**. From the **E**dit menu, select **M**ark Block.

3. Move the cursor to mark the block of text you want to copy into the Clipboard.

4. Press **F10**. From the **E**dit menu, select **C**opy To Clipboard.

   The text remains in the Clipboard until you replace it or end the program.

To cut text to the Clipboard or erase a block of text

1. Move the cursor to where you want to begin cutting or erasing text.

2. Press **F10**. From the **E**dit menu, select **M**ark Block.

3. Move the cursor to mark the block of text you want to cut to the Clipboard or to erase.

4. Press **F10**. From the **E**dit menu, select Cu**T** To Clipboard.

To paste text from the Clipboard

1. Move the cursor to where you want to paste the text from the Clipboard.

2. Press **F10**. From the **E**dit menu, select **P**aste.

To insert a file

1. Move the cursor to where you want to insert a file.

2. Press **F10**. From the **E**dit menu, select **I**nsert File.

3. Select the file you want to insert from the File Load dialog box.

4. To load the file, select **L**oad by pressing **Alt-L**.

To delete all text

1. Press **F10**. From the **E**dit menu, select **D**elete All Text.

2. Select **O**K to confirm the deletion or **C**ancel to abandon the operation.

To use the Goto command

1. Press **F10**. From the **E**dit menu, select **G**oto.

2. Type the line number to which you want to go. Press **Enter**.

3. Select **O**K.

To use the Find command

1. Press **F10**. From the **S**earch menu, select **F**ind.

   or

   Press **F6**.

2. In the Find dialog box, type the text you want to find. Press **Enter**.

3. To select one of the following options, press **Tab**:

   Case Sensitive finds exact matches only. For example, if you search for "the," the Clipboard ignores "The."

Command Reference

Whole Words Only searches for entire words only. For example, if you search for "his," Clipboard ignores "history."

4. Select **F**ind by pressing **Alt-F**.

5. To find the next occurrence of the same text, press **F7**.

To use the Replace command

1. Press **F10**. From the **S**earch menu, select **R**eplace.

2. Type the characters you want to replace in the Search For box. Press **Enter**.

3. Type the replacement characters in the Replace With box. Press **Enter**.

4. Press **Tab** to select any of the following options:

   Replace One Time
   Replace All
   Verify Before Replace
   Case Sensitive
   Whole Words Only

5. To perform the replacement, select **R**eplace by pressing **Alt-R**.

6. After making all replacements, select **Cancel**.

To check the spelling of a word

1. Position the cursor in the word you want to check.

2. Press **F10**. From the **E**dit menu, select Spellcheck **W**ord.

3. Select one of the following options for each misspelled word:

   Ignore disregards the word.

   Correct displays the Word Correction dialog box. Select the correct word from the list of possible words, then select **A**ccept. To enter your own correction, press **Tab** to select the text box, type the correct spelling, press **Enter**, then select **A**ccept.

Add adds the word to the dictionary.

Quit exits the Spellcheck feature.

To check the spelling in a screen

1. Move the cursor to the screen you want to check.

2. Press **F10**. From the **E**dit menu, select Spellcheck **S**creen.

3. Select **I**gnore, **C**orrect, **A**dd, or **Q**uit for any misspelled words.

To check the spelling in a file

1. Press **F10**. From the **E**dit menu, select Spellcheck **F**ile.

   or

   Press **F8**.

2. Select **I**gnore, **C**orrect, **A**dd, or **Q**uit for any misspelled words.

To set the page layout

1. Press **F10**. From the **C**ontrols menu, select **P**age Layout.

2. Set the margins and the paper size and width.

3. Select **O**K by pressing **Alt-O**.

To create a header or footer

1. Press **F10**. From the **C**ontrols menu, select **H**eader/Footer.

2. Type the header or footer in the Page Header Footer dialog box. To print page numbers, use the **#** symbol in the header or footer.

3. Select **O**K by pressing **Alt-O**.

To set or delete tabs on the tab ruler

1. Press **F10**. From the **C**ontrols menu, select Tab **R**uler Edit.

2. Press the **left arrow** or **right arrow** to move the cursor on the tab ruler.

3. Press **Ins** to set a tab, press **Del** to delete a tab, or press **Esc** to continue working.

To set evenly spaced tabs

1. Press **F10**. From the **C**ontrols menu, select Tab **R**uler Edit.

2. To specify the spacing between tabs, type a number (of horizontal positions) between 3 and 29.

3. Press **Esc** to continue working.

To change to overtype mode

Press **F10**. From the **C**ontrols menu, select **O**vertype Mode.

or

Press **Ins**.

Check that INS does not appear in the upper right corner of the window.

To display control characters

Press **F10**. From the **C**ontrols menu, select **C**ontrol Char Display.

To turn on Wordwrap

Press **F10**. From the **C**ontrols menu, select **W**ordwrap.

To turn on Auto Indent

Press **F10**. From the **C**ontrols menu, select **A**uto Indent.

To save a Notepads setup

Press **F10**. From the **C**ontrols menu, select **S**ave Setup.

Note

If PC Tools Desktop is memory-resident, you can access Notepads from within other applications using the Desktop hotkey.

Outlines

Beg / Int / Adv   *DESKTOP*

Purpose
Enables you to enter text in outline form.

To create a new outline

1. From the main **D**esktop menu, select **O**utlines.

2. Type the name of the outline in the File Load dialog box. The outline file name must have the extension OUT.

3. Select **N**ew by pressing **Alt-N**.

4. Type the text. Each line is called a headline. Use **Tab** to establish the different levels in an outline.

To change the level of a headline

1. Press **F10**. From the **F**ile menu, select **H**eadlines.

2. To promote a headline (to place it on a higher level and move it to the left), select **P**romote.

3. To demote a headline (to place it on a lower level and move it to the right), select **D**emote.

To change the display of headlines

1. Press **F10**. From the **F**ile menu, select **H**eadlines.

2. Select from the following options:

Expand Current	Displays headlines below the current headline.
Expand **A**ll	Displays all headlines.
Show Level	Hides all headlines below the current level.
Collapse Current	Hides all headlines below the current headline.
Main Headline Only	Hides all headlines below the main level.

To save an outline

1. Press **F10**. From the **F**ile menu, select **S**ave.

2. Type the file name. The extension must be OUT. Press **Enter**.

3. Press **Tab** to select any of the following options:

PC Tools Desktop	Saves the file in a PC Tools Desktop file format.
ASCII	Saves the file as a regular ASCII file.
Make backup File	Creates a second (backup) file with the same file name, but with the extension BAK.

4. To save the file, select **S**ave by pressing **Alt-S**.

Park Disk Heads

Int / Adv   *PCSHELL*

Purpose

Parks the read/write head of the hard drive over an unused portion of the hard disk.

To park hard disk drive heads

1. Select the **D**isk menu by pressing **Alt-D**, then select **P**ark Disk Heads.

   The hard disk head is parked at the highest unused cylinder on the drive.

2. Turn off the power to your computer.

Note

This command prevents the loss of data or damage to your hard disk that could occur if the head accidentally touches the surface of the hard disk. Be sure to use this command before you move your computer.

PC-Cache

Beg / Int / Adv　　　　　　　　　　　　　　**PC-CACHE**

Purpose

Stores the most frequently used data from disk in memory and speeds hard and floppy disk access by reducing the number of times your computer has to wait for the disk when reading and writing data.

To run PC-Cache

Type **PC-CACHE** at the DOS prompt, then press **Enter**.

You can select which drives to process; where to load the data in memory; whether to use regular, extended, or expanded memory; how much memory to allot to the cache; and other parameter options. These parameter options are summarized in PC-Cache's help display.

To display help for PC-Cache options

Type **PC-CACHE /?** at the DOS prompt, then press **Enter**.

To run PC-Cache when you boot your computer

Enter **PC-CACHE** and any parameter options you want to use into your AUTOEXEC.BAT file.

PC Config

Beg / Int / Adv　　　　　　　　　　　　　　*PCCONFIG*

Purpose

Selects colors and shadings for all PC Tools displays, whether to use graphics or text displays, and keyboard and mouse parameters.

To run PC Config

Type **PCCONFIG** at the DOS prompt, then press **Enter**.

Command Reference

To configure colors

1. Select **C**olor from the PC Config main menu.
2. Select **S**cheme.

   A list of color schemes appears. This list includes PC Tools' original color schemes and any other color schemes you have saved.

3. Select a color scheme. Select **O**K.
4. To modify the color scheme, select C**A**tegory.

   A list of the categories of displayed items appears.

5. Select a category of displayed items. Press **Enter**.
6. Select E**L**ement.

   A list of the elements of the selected category appears.

7. Select an element of the category. Press **Enter**.
8. To change the color of that element, select **C**olor.

   Lists of background and foreground colors appear.

9. Use the **left arrow** or **right arrow** to select the background or foreground list. Use the **up arrow** or **down arrow** to select background and foreground colors. Press **Enter**.
10. Repeat steps 4 through 9 for each display element you want to change.
11. Select **O**K.

To configure the display

1. Select **D**isplay from the PC Config main menu.
2. Select **G**raphics Mode or **T**ext Mode. **G**raphics Mode is available only if you have a VGA or EGA display adapter.
3. If you have a CGA monitor, you can select **F**ast Video On CGA. If the screen snows or flickers, turn this option off.
4. Select the number of lines of text to display on screen. If you have a VGA display adapter, 28- and 50-line displays are available. If you have an EGA display adapter, a 43-line display is available.

5. Select **O**K.

To configure the keyboard

1. Select **K**eyboard from the PC Config main menu.

2. Select **E**nable Keyboard Speed.

3. Select the Rate and Delay for the keyboard. Rate determines how rapidly a keystroke repeats when you hold a key. Delay determines how long you must hold a key before it begins to repeat.

4. Select **O**K.

To configure the mouse

1. Select **M**ouse from the PC Config main menu.

2. Select the options you want to use:

   Fast Mouse **R**eset provides optimal mouse performance. If the mouse stops working, turn this option off.

   Left Handed Mouse exchanges left and right mouse key functions (for left-handed people). This option may be confusing, because instructions about using the mouse refer to the keys in the usual configuration.

   Disable Mouse is the option to use if the mouse driver is incompatible or the mouse does not work.

   Graphics **M**ouse displays the mouse cursor as an arrow.

3. Select the mouse speed.

4. Select **O**K.

PC Format

Beg / Int / Adv   ***PCFORMAT***

Purpose

Enables you to format disks, initializing every track on the disk so that your computer recognizes the disk and uses it to store your data files. You also can create system bootable disks with this command.

To format a data disk

1. Insert a blank disk into drive A or B.

2. Type **PCFORMAT** at the DOS prompt. Press **Enter**.

   You can add regular DOS switches to this command line. For example, **PCFORMAT A /S** formats the A disk and copies the system to that disk.

3. In the Drive Selection dialog box, select the drive holding the blank disk. Select **O**K to continue.

4. Select format options from the Select Format Options dialog box. For more information, see *Format Data Disk*.

5. After selecting options, select **O**K to proceed with formatting your disk. The Formatting dialog box displays the status.

6. Select **O**K, then select **C**ancel, then select E**X**it by pressing **Alt-X**, then select **O**K.

Caution

This command may destroy all files or data already stored on your disk. Unlike the DOS FORMAT command, disks formatted with this command may not be recoverable.

PC Secure

Beg / Int / Adv   *PCSECURE*

Purpose

Adds a high level of security to sensitive or confidential files stored on your computer's disks by encrypting, decrypting, compressing, and hiding files.

To run PC Secure

1. Type **PCSECURE** at the DOS prompt, then press **Enter**.

   To use DOD-standard encryption, type the command **PCSECURE /G** at the DOS prompt, then press **Enter**.

2. PC Secure prompts you to enter a Master Key password. This password enables you to decrypt your encrypted files even if you forget a particular file's password.

To select encryption options

1. Select the **O**ptions menu.

2. Toggle on or off the following options:

Full DES Encryption	Uses DES standards for encryption.
Quick Encryption	Encrypts the file once.
Compression	Compresses the file.
One Key	Uses the same password for all files encrypted during the session.
Hidden	Turns on the file's Hidden attribute.
Read Only	Turns on the file's Read Only attribute.
Delete Original File	Destroys the original file after encryption.
Expert mode	Disables the Master Key.

3. To save this configuration, select **S**ave Configuration.

To encrypt (scramble) a file or all files in a directory

1. Press **F10**. From the **F**ile menu, select **E**ncrypt File.

   or

   Press **F4**.

2. Select the drive and directory using **Tab** and the cursor keys.

3. In the File Selection dialog box, select the file you want to encrypt. Select **E**ncrypt by pressing **Alt-E**.

or

Select **D**irectory by pressing **Alt-D**, then select **O**K.

4. Type your password in the Password dialog box.

5. Type your password again to confirm it.

   The Progress box displays selected options and file statistics. A message indicates when encryption is complete.

6. Select **O**K.

To decrypt (unscramble) a file or all files in a directory

1. Press **F10**. From the **F**ile menu, select **D**ecrypt.

   or

   Press **F5**.

2. Select the drive and directory using **Tab** and the cursor keys.

3. In the File Selection dialog box, select the file you want to decrypt. Select De**C**rypt by pressing **Alt-C**.

   or

   Select **D**irectory by pressing **Alt-D**, then select **O**K.

4. Type your password in the dialog box.

   The Progress box displays selected options and file statistics. A message indicates when decryption is complete.

5. Select **O**K.

Cautions

Do not encrypt system files or their directories. It is also dangerous to encrypt files with COM or EXE extensions.

If you operate the program improperly, the data you encrypt may be lost forever. For example, you must remember your password, or you can never retrieve the data.

PC Shell

Beg / Int / Adv *PCSHELL*

Purpose

Copies, moves, deletes, edits, maps, recovers, and compares files, directories, and disks. PC Shell also provides information about files, disks, and the system.

To start PC Shell

Type **PCSHELL** at the DOS prompt and press **Enter**.

If your computer has enough memory, PC Shell loads.

To load PC Shell as a memory-resident TSR

Type **PCSHELL /R** at the DOS prompt and press **Enter**. Enter the PC Shell by pressing **Ctrl-Esc**.

PC Shell Keyboard Shortcuts:

Key(s)	Action
F1	Displays context-sensitive help.
F2	Activates Quick View.
F3	Cancels the command, exits the dialog box, or exits PC Shell.
F4	Unselects the selected files.
F5	Copies the selected files.
F6	Changes file sorting and display options.
F7	Locates files.
F8	Zooms the current window.
F9	Selects files.
F10	Displays the Main menu or Program List.
Ctrl-A	Selects the A drive.

Key(s)	Action
Ctrl-B	Selects the B drive.
Ctrl-C	Selects the C drive.
Ctrl-Enter	Runs the selected program or associated application.
Alt-space bar	Sizes/Moves the window.
Ins	Displays a Dual File List.
Del	Displays a Single File List.
Tab	Selects options or buttons in a dialog box.
Enter	Selects a highlighted box.
Esc	Cancels the command, exits the dialog box, or exits PC Shell.
Alt-*highlighted letter*	Executes an option or command.

Print

Int / Adv　　　　　　　　　　　　　　*PCSHELL*

Purpose

Prints the contents of a file or files.

To print files

1. Select the files you want to print.
2. Select the File menu by pressing **Alt-F**, then select Print.
3. To print a file, select Print File.
4. Select a print option in the File Print dialog box:

Print As Standard **T**ext File prints the file as a standard ASCII text file.

Print File Using PC Shell Print **O**ptions defines the page layout for printing, then prints the file as a standard text file.

Dump Each Sector In ASCII And HEX prints sectors in ASCII and hexadecimal format.

5. Select **P**rint to continue.

6. If you selected Print File Using PC Shell Print Options (in step 4), select any options in the File Print dialog box:

   Lines Per Page specifies the number of lines on a page.

   Extra Spaces Between Lines specifies the number of blank lines between printed lines.

   Margin Lines Top And Bottom specifies the number of lines for top and bottom margins.

   Left Margin specifies the first print position of each line.

   Right Margin specifies the last print position of each line.

   Page **H**eaders prints a header on each page. This option prompts you to enter the header text.

   Page **F**ooters prints a footer on each page. This option prompts you to enter the footer text.

   Page **N**umbers numbers each page.

   Stop Between Pages stops printing after each page. Used for printing single sheets.

   Eject Last Page ejects the last page printed.

7. After selecting options, select **P**rint to start printing the selected files.

Command Reference

Print File List

Int / Adv **PCSHELL**

Purpose

Prints a complete file list for any selected subdirectory. The list contains the name, size, number of disk clusters, date, time, and attributes of each file.

To print a list of files

1. Select the File menu by pressing **Alt-F**, then select **P**rint.

2. Select Print File **L**ist.

Quick File View

Beg / Int / Adv **PCSHELL**

Purpose

Enables you to view a file in its native format in a zoomed window. Many formats are available, including popular word processors, spreadsheets, and databases.

To view a file

1. Select the file you want to view.

2. Select the **F**ile menu by pressing **Alt-F**, then select **V**iew File Contents.

   or

   Press **F2**.

Quick Run

Beg / Int / Adv **PCSHELL**

Purpose

Enables you to select whether PC Shell frees memory before running a selected program.

To toggle on or off Quick Run

Select the **O**ptions menu by pressing **Alt-O**, then select **Q**uick Run (the default is off).

If Quick Run is on, PC Shell does not free memory before running programs. Programs start quickly, but if a program is too large for the available memory, it does not run at all.

If Quick Run is off, PC Shell frees memory before running programs. Programs start more slowly, but the free memory may enable you to run large programs.

Note

The Quick Run command is available only when you run PC Shell from the DOS command line.

Recalling Past Commands

Beg / Int / Adv   *PCSHELL*

Purpose

Recalls the last 16 commands that you entered on the DOS command line. You must have PC Shell running and the DOS command line displayed.

To use the DOS command line in PC Shell

1. Press **Tab** to select the DOS prompt.
2. Enter a DOS command, then press **Enter**.

To recall a past command

1. Press **Ctrl-left arrow** to display the preceding DOS command (up to the last 16 commands) on the DOS command line.

    Press **Ctrl-right arrow** to display the next DOS command on the DOS command line (to move forward in the list of previous commands).

2. When you display the DOS command you want to use, press **Enter** to start that DOS command.

Remove PC Shell

Beg / Int / Adv **PCSHELL**

Purpose

Removes the PC Shell program from memory when PC Shell is running in TSR mode.

To remove PC shell

1. Press **Ctrl-Esc** from the DOS prompt (to run PC Shell in TSR mode).

2. Select the **S**pecial menu by pressing **Alt-S**, then select **R**emove PC Shell.

3. To continue, select **R**emove.

    or

    Type **KILL** at any DOS prompt and press **Enter**.

Note

If PC Shell was the last TSR program you loaded, **R**emove PC Shell also removes PC Tools Desktop from your computer's memory. If you loaded other TSR programs after loading PC Shell, this command may have undesirable results. To avoid problems, remove the other TSR programs before using this command.

Rename File

Beg / Int / Adv **PCSHELL**

Purpose

Enables you to rename a file or files.

To rename a file

1. Select the file(s) you want to rename.

2. Select the **F**ile menu by pressing **Alt-F**, then select Re**N**ame.

3. If you selected more than one file, select **G**lobal to rename all selected files according to a pattern or select **S**ingle to rename one file at a time. Then select **O**K.

    If you select **S**ingle, the current file name and extension appear in the File Rename dialog box.

4. Select one of the following options:

    To rename the file, select **R**ename by pressing **Alt-R**. Type the new file name.

    To skip the current file and display the next selected file, select **N**ext File by pressing **Alt-N**.

    To end the renaming and return to the main PC Shell screen, select **C**ancel by pressing **Alt-C**.

Rename Volume

Int / Adv   *PCSHELL, DM*

Purpose

Renames the disk volume label.

To rename a volume

1. Select the disk you want to rename. Press **Ctrl-A**, **Ctrl-B**, or **Ctrl-C** to select drive A, B, or C, respectively.

    or

    Click the drive letter in the drive line of the main PC Shell screen.

2. Select the **D**isk menu by pressing **Alt-D**, then select **R**ename Volume.

3. Type the new volume name (no more than 11 characters) in the Disk Rename dialog box. Press **Enter**.

4. Select **R**ename by pressing **Alt-R**.

Run

Beg / Int / Adv　　　　　　　　　　　　　　*PCSHELL*

Purpose

Enables you to run a program or application associated with a selected data file if the program or associated application is listed in the Program List.

To run a program file from the File List window

1. Select a program file in the File List window. Program file names must have a COM, EXE, or BAT extension.

2. Select the **F**ile menu by pressing **Alt-F**, then select **R**un.

   or

   Press **Ctrl-Enter**.

   The Run dialog box appears.

3. Enter any parameters, then select **O**K by pressing **Alt-O**.

To run a program from the Program List

1. Select the Program List by pressing **F10**.

2. Select a program from the Program List.

3. Press **Enter**.

To run an application associated with a data file

1. Select a data file in the File List window. The extension of the file name must be associated with an application from the program list.

2. Select the **F**ile menu by pressing **Alt-F**, then select **R**un.

   or

   Press **Ctrl-Enter**.

   The Run dialog box appears.

3. Enter any parameters, then select **O**K by pressing **Alt-O**.

To run a program using the mouse
Double-click the program in the File List window.

Save Configuration File

Beg / Int / Adv   *PCSHELL*

Purpose

Saves selected PC Shell options so that you do not need to enter configuration commands each time you use PC Shell.

To save the new configuration
From the **O**ptions menu, select S**A**ve Configuration File.

Screen Blanker

DATAMON

Purpose

Clears the screen when the computer is idle for a specified period of time (to prevent "burn in" on the surface of the monitor if the same image is displayed for too long). You also can clear the screen manually to prevent people from seeing sensitive information.

To turn on Screen Blanker

1. Select **S**creen Blanker.
2. Select **L**oad Screen Blanker.
3. Select from the following options:

   Blank Screen After   Enables you to enter the number of minutes the computer must be idle before the screen blanks.

Command Reference

Password   Enables you to enter a
                     password. When the screen
                     blanks, enter that password to
                     restore the display.

Hotkey   Enables you to enter a hotkey
                     combination used to blank
                     the screen manually.

4. Select **O**K.

To blank the screen manually

Press the hotkey. The default is **Alt-Enter**.

Search Disk

Int / Adv   *PCSHELL*

Purpose

Searches entire disk for ASCII text or Hex character strings.

To search a disk for a string

1. Select the disk you want to search. Press **Ctrl-A**, **Ctrl-B**, or **Ctrl-C** to select drive A, B, or C, respectively.

   or

   Click the drive letter on the drive line of the main PC Shell screen.

2. Select the **D**isk menu by pressing **Alt-D**, then select **S**earch.

3. In the Disk Search dialog box, type the string you want to find. The maximum search string length is 32 characters.

   To search for ASCII characters, type the character string on the ASCII default line. The ASCII search is not case-sensitive (entering "hello" also finds "HELLO").

To search for Hex values, select **H**ex by pressing **Alt-H**, then type the Hex values on the Hex default line. The Hex search is case-sensitive. If you type an invalid Hex value, PC Shell beeps.

4. To begin the search, select **O**K by pressing **Alt-O**.

   PC Tools displays any matching strings; otherwise, the following message appears:

   ```
   The search string was NOT found
   ```

5. For each matching string, select from the following options:

Name	Displays the name of the file containing the text string.
Edit	Enables you to edit the text string as with the **H**ex Edit File command.
OK	Continues searching the disk for another matching string.
Cancel	Ends the search.

6. To end the search, press **Esc**.

Search File

Int / Adv　　　　　　　　　　　　　　　　*PCSHELL*

Purpose

Enables you to search files for ASCII text or Hex character strings.

To search a file

1. Select the file(s) you want to search. PC Shell searches the files in the order you select them.

2. Select the **F**ile menu by pressing **Alt-F**, then select Searc**H**.

Command Reference

3. In the File Search dialog box, type the string you want to find. The maximum length of a search string is 32 characters.

   To search for ASCII characters, type the character string on the ASCII default line. The ASCII search is not case-sensitive (entering "hello" also finds "HELLO").

   To search for Hex values, select **H**ex by pressing **Alt-H**, then type the Hex values on the Hex default line. The Hex search is case-sensitive. If you type an invalid Hex value, PC Shell beeps.

4. After typing the string you want to find, you also can select one of the following options:

   All Files (**Alt-A**) searches for the string in all files.

   Selected Files (**Alt-S**) searches for the string in selected files only.

   Unselected Files (**Alt-U**) searches for the string in unselected files only.

   Se**L**ect File and Continue (**Alt-L**) selects any file with matching text and continues to look for matching strings.

   Pause Search (**Alt-P**) temporarily suspends the search if the string is found.

5. To begin the search, select **O**K by pressing **Alt-O**.

   PC Tools displays any matching strings; otherwise, the following message appears:

   ```
   The search string was NOT found
   ```

6. For each matching string, select one of the following options:

   Next File skips to the next file.

   Edit enables you to edit the file.

7. To end the search, press **Esc**.

Setup Configuration

Beg / Int / Adv   *PCSHELL*

Purpose

Controls the screen's appearance and the way PC Shell displays your files and lists.

To change the user level

1. Select the **O**ptions menu by pressing **Alt-O**, then select Change **U**ser Level.

2. If prompted, type the password.

3. Select **B**eginner, **I**ntermediate, or **A**dvanced User Mode, then select **O**K.

To change displayed items

1. Select the **V**iew menu by pressing **Alt-V**, then select **C**ustom List Configure.

2. Select from the following the items you want to display:

   Tree List
   File List
   Program List
   View Window
   Background **M**at
   DOS Command Line

   You now can enter any DOS command at the DOS prompt.

To set the screen colors

1. Select the **O**ptions menu by pressing **Alt-O**, then select C**O**lors.

   PC Shell runs the PC CONFIG function.

2. Select **S**cheme.

   A list of color schemes appears. This list includes PC Tools' original color schemes and any other color schemes you have saved.

Command Reference

3. Select a color scheme. Select **OK**.
4. To modify the color scheme, select C**A**tegory.

   A list of the categories of displayed items appears.

5. Select a category of displayed items. Press **Enter**.
6. Select E**L**ement.

   A list of the elements of the selected category appears.

7. Select an element of the category. Press **Enter**.
8. To change the color of that element, select **C**olor.

   Lists of background and foreground colors appear.

9. Use the **left arrow** or **right arrow** to select the background or foreground list. Use the **up arrow** or **down arrow** to select background and foreground colors. Press **Enter**.
10. Repeat steps 4 through 9 for each display element you want to change.
11. Select **O**K.

To set the date or time

1. Select the **V**iew menu by pressing **Alt-V**, then select Set Date/**T**ime.
2. Type the new date in the Set Date And Time dialog box. You must enter the date in the MM-DD-YY format. Press **Enter** to accept the new date and move to the time option.
3. Type the new time. You must enter the time in the HH:MM format. Press **Enter** to accept the new time.
4. To set the new date and time on your computer, select **S**et by pressing **Alt-S**.

   PC Shell sets the new time and date and the program returns to the main PC Shell screen.

To define the function keys

1. Select the **O**ptions menu by pressing **Alt-O**, then select Define Function **K**eys.

   The Define Function Keys dialog box appears.

2. If prompted, type the password.

3. Use the **up arrow** or **down arrow** to select the function key you want to change. Press **Enter**.

   You cannot reassign **F1**, **F3**, or **F10**. **F1** is reserved to access Help, **F3** is reserved to Exit, and **F10** is reserved to access the PC Shell menu system.

4. Use the **up arrow** or **down arrow** to scroll through the list of available functions. Press **Enter** to assign the selected function to the selected function key.

5. Select **U**pdate to accept the function key assignment or **R**eset to return to original key definitions.

Show File Information

Beg / Int / Adv *PCSHELL*

Purpose

Lists the file name, the extension, the file path, any attributes assigned to the file, the last date and time the file was accessed, the file length, the total number of clusters the file occupies, the starting cluster number, and total files in the directory.

To display file information

1. Select the file(s) about which you want more information.

2. Select the **O**ptions menu by pressing **Alt-O**, then select **S**how Information.

3. If you select more than one file, select **N**ext File to display file information about the next file.

4. To return to the main PC Shell Screen, select **O**K.

Command Reference

Size/Move Window

Beg / Int / Adv **PCSHELL**

Purpose

Sizes or moves the active Tree List window or the File List window.

To size a window

1. Use **Tab** to select the window you want to size.
2. Press **Alt-space bar**.
3. Select **S**ize from the Window Control dialog box.
4. Use the arrow keys to resize the window.

   The upper left corner of the window remains stationary while the lower right corner of the window moves.

5. Press **Enter** when you finish sizing the window.

To size a window using the mouse

1. Click the window you want to size.
2. Position the mouse cursor in the size box in the lower right corner of the window.
3. Drag the size box to resize the window.

   The upper left corner of the window remains stationary while the lower right corner of the window moves.

4. Release the mouse button when you finish sizing the window.

To move a window

1. Press **Tab** to select the window you want to move.
2. Press **Alt-space bar**.
3. Select **M**ove from the Window Control dialog box.
4. Use the arrow keys to move the window.

   The size of the window does not change when you move the window; only the on-screen position of the window changes.

5. Press **Enter** when you finish moving the window.

To move a window using the mouse

1. Position the mouse cursor in the window and click the mouse button once to activate the window.

2. Position the mouse cursor in the top window border. Do not position the mouse cursor in the close box (located in the upper left corner of the window).

3. Drag the window to its new location.

4. Release the mouse button when you finish moving the window.

Sort Files in Directory

Int / Adv　　　　　　　　　　　　　　　*PCSHELL*

Purpose

Sorts the files in the selected directory. After you sort the files, you can view the list of sorted files and update the list of files on your disk.

To sort a directory

1. Select the drive where the directory you want to sort is located. Press **Ctrl-A**, **Ctrl-B**, or **Ctrl-C** to select drive A, B, or C, respectively.

   or

   Click the drive letter on the drive line of the main PC Shell screen.

2. Select the directory you want to sort.

3. Select the **D**isk menu by pressing **Alt-D**, then select Sor**T** Files In Directory.

4. Select one of the following sort types:

   1 By Name   Sorts by file name.

   2 By Extension   Sorts by file extension.

Command Reference

> **3** By Size — Sorts by number of bytes in the file.
>
> **4** By Date/time — Sorts by file date and time.
>
> **5** By Select Number — Sorts by the number associated with the selected files.

5. Select the sort method:

   6 Ascending

   7 Descending

6. Select **S**ort.

7. To see the new sort order, select **V**iew.

8. Press any key to return to the Directory Sort dialog box.

9. To save this sort order, select **U**pdate.

   After updating, the program returns to the main PC Shell screen.

Speed Search

Beg / Int / Adv   *PCSHELL*

Purpose

Enables quick selection of directories from the Tree List window.

To select a directory with Speed Search

1. Use **Tab** to select the Tree List window.

2. Type last part of the directory name. For example, to select C:\WP\FILES\REPORTS, type **REPORTS**.

   Speed Search moves to the next directory in the list that matches the name you type.

3. Press **Enter** to select the directory.

To start the search from the top of the list
   Press **Home**.

System Info

Beg / Int / Adv   ***PCSHELL, SI***

Purpose

Displays information about your computer system and network.

To display general system information

1. Select the **S**pecial menu by pressing **Alt-S**, then select **S**ystem Info.

   PC Shell runs the SI function. The SI function displays information about system type, operating system, video adapter, I/O Ports, keyboard, mouse, CMOS, network, and drives.

2. To return to the main PC Shell screen after reviewing the information about your computer, press **F3** and select **O**K.

To display computer system type information

Select S**Y**stem Type. PC Shell's display includes CPU type, coprocessor, bus size, bus type, date of BIOS, and ID bytes.

To display operating system information

Select **O**perating System. PC Shell's display includes DOS version, OEM identification, and serial number.

To display video adapter information

Select **V**ideo Adapter. PC Shell's display includes type of video adapter and display, video memory size, active video mode, character height in pixels, CGA emulation status, and maximum number of scan lines.

To display I/O port information

Select I/O Po**R**ts. PC Shell's display includes number of ports, type of ports, names, and base addresses.

Command Reference

To display keyboard and mouse information

Select **K**eyboard/Mouse. PC Shell's display includes type of keyboard, keyboard interrupt support, enhanced and extended functionality status, mouse type, revision level, and IRQ number.

To display CMOS information

Select **C**MOS. PC Shell's display includes drives, memory, CMOS battery status, and disk controller status.

To display network information

Select Ne**T**work. PC Shell's display includes servers, number of users, current user, login time and date, and connection number.

To display drive summary information

Select Dr**I**ve Summary. PC Shell's display includes number and types of drives, capacity, and current default directory.

To display memory information

To display conventional memory, select Co**N**ventional Memory. PC Shell's display shows the contents of conventional RAM.

To display extended memory, select E**X**tended Memory. PC Shell's display shows bytes available in extended memory.

To display expanded memory, select Ex**P**anded Memory. PC Shell's display shows total pages of memory, number in use, number available, total bytes, number in use, and number available.

Telecommunications

Beg / Int / Adv   *DESKTOP*

Purpose

Enables you to communicate with other computers via a modem.

The Telecommunications window

The information in the Telecommunications window includes the following:

- COM Port identifies the communications port your computer uses to send information to your modem.

- Name contains a label assigned to each entry displayed in the Telecommunications window. The name is usually the name of the computer service or someone to whom you regularly send files. To select an entry quickly, type the number to the left of the name.

- Number displays the phone number you want your computer to dial. If no number appears, Telecommunication asks for the number each time you dial the entry.

- Baud sets the speed at which communication takes place. The baud rate should match the speed of your computer and modem.

- Duplex determines how the computers handle the transmitted data.

- Parity/Data/Stop (PDS) bits set the character format used during data transmission. Improper settings prevent normal communications.

- Script File contains the name of any script file used for automatic dialing and logging on to another computer.

To start Telecommunications

1. From the Desktop main menu, select Telecommunications.

2. Select Modem Telecommunications or Electronic Mail.

Modem Telecommunications

The Modem Telecommunications capability enables you to use your modem to dial electronic bulletin boards or on-line services, to upload and download files, and to send and receive information.

Command Reference

To load an existing phone directory

1. Press **F10**. From the **F**ile menu, select **L**oad.
2. Press **Tab** to select the name of the phone directory you want to use.
3. To select **L**oad, press **Alt-L**.

To load a new phone directory

1. Press **F10**. From the **F**ile menu, select **L**oad.
2. Type the name of a new phone directory (use the TEL extension).
3. To select **N**ew, press **Alt-N**.

To save a phone directory

1. Press **F10**. From the **F**ile menu, select **S**ave.
2. Type a file name, then press **Enter**.
3. Select **S**ave again by pressing **Alt-S**.

To change phone directory parameters

1. Press the **up arrow** or **down arrow** to select the line you want to edit.
2. Press **F10**. From the **E**dit menu, select **E**dit Entry.

   or

   Press **F6**.

3. Press **Tab** to select any of the following communications parameters:

   Name is the name (up to 50 characters) of the person, company, or computer service you are calling.

   Database is the name of a PC Tools database containing information you may use during the communications session.

   Field 1 and Field 2 are fields in the specified database. You can use Database, Field 1, and Field 2 to send information to other subscribers.

   Phone Number is the phone number and any additional commands used by the modem to dial the phone. Leave the phone number text box empty if you want to make communication settings only.

Script is the file name and SCR extension for any script file containing commands for automatic dialing.

User ID is your user ID for logging on to information services.

Password is your password for logging on to information services.

4. In the Next Screen, use Tab to select any of the following parameters:

Baud Rate is the transmission speed. The higher the number, the faster the transmission. Your modem determines how high the number can be.

Parity specifies how characters are transferred. Both your computer and the computer you are calling must have the same settings.

Terminal enables your computer to emulate a teletype terminal.

Flow Control controls the flow of data between two computers and lessens the chance of data loss. The setting must be the same for both computers. Select XON/XOFF or None.

EOL Receive enables you to select Add LF (add a line feed), Add CR (add a carriage return), or None.

EOL Send. Consult the subscription service manual to select how the end of each line is processed.

Data Bits specify how characters are transferred. Both your computer and the computer you are calling must have the same settings.

Stop Bits specify how characters are transferred. Both your computer and the computer you are calling must have the same settings.

Duplex enables you to select Full or Half. Most systems are full duplex. If you cannot see what you are typing during communications, change the setting to Half. If you see two of each character, change the setting to Full.

5. To accept the new settings, select OK.

Command Reference

To add a new entry to a phone directory

1. Press **F10**. From the **E**dit menu, select **C**reate New Entry.

2. Press **Tab** to select any of the communications parameters and make the appropriate entries.

3. To accept the new settings, select **O**K.

To remove an entry from a phone directory

1. Select the entry you want to remove using the **up arrow** or **down arrow**.

2. Press **F10**. From the **E**dit menu, select **R**emove Entry.

To dial another computer automatically

1. Select the computer you want to call using the **up arrow** or **down arrow**.

2. Press **F10**. From the **A**ctions menu, select **D**ial.

   or

   Press **Enter**.

   or

   Press **F7**.

   or

   Double-click the entry.

   If no phone number appears on the line, a dialog box appears, and you must type the phone number.

3. To accept the phone number, select **O**K.

To hang up the phone

Press **F10**. From the **A**ctions menu, select **H**angup Phone.

To receive an ASCII or XMODEM file

1. Press **F10**. From the **R**eceive menu, select **A**SCII or **X**MODEM.

2. Type the name of the file you want to receive.

3. To receive the file, select **S**ave.

4. After receiving the file, press **Esc**.

To send an ASCII or XMODEM file

1. Press **F10**. From the **S**end menu, select **A**SCII or **X**MODEM.

2. Press **Tab** to select the file you want to send.

3. Press **Alt-L** to select **L**oad.

To end a transfer

Press **F10**. From the **A**ctions menu, select **E**nd Transfer.

Electronic Mail

The Electronic Mail capability enables you to send and receive electronic mail on MCI Mail, CompuServe, or EasyLink services.

To start Electronic Mail

1. From the **D**esktop main menu, select **T**elecommunications.

2. Select **E**lectronic Mail.

To set up or change the electronic mail service

1. From the **S**etup menu, select **M**ail Service.

2. Select MCI Mail, CompuServe, EasyLink, or No Service.

3. Select Co**N**figure.

The following parameters are available:

Phone Number is the phone number and any additional commands used by the modem to dial the phone. Leave the phone number text box empty if you want to make communications settings only.

User ID is your user ID for logging on to information services.

Password is your password for logging on to information services.

Baud Rate is the transmission speed. The higher the number, the faster the transmission. Your modem determines how high the number can be.

Dialing enables you to select touch-tone or pulse (rotary) dialing.

Port enables you to select the I/O port where your modem is connected.

4. After selecting parameters, select OK.

To dial the mail service and download electronic mail

From the Actions menu, select Read Mail Now.

or

Press F7.

To create electronic mail messages

1. From the Actions menu, select Create Mail Message.

    or

    Press F8.

2. Type the message.

    or

    If the text already exists in a file, select the File menu by pressing Alt-F, select the file you want to load, then select Load by pressing Alt-L.

    You can edit files as in Notepads.

3. After creating the message, select the File menu by pressing Alt-F, then select Save or select Send Electronic Mail.

To view the In box

From the View menu, select View Inbox.

or

Press F4.

To view the Out box

From the View menu, select View Outbox.

or

Press F5.

To view the mail sent

From the **V**iew menu, select View **S**ent.

or

Press **F6**.

Undelete File

Int / Adv **PCSHELL, UNDELETE**

Purpose

Recovers files you have unintentionally deleted or erased and subdirectories you have removed.

To start Undelete

Select the **F**ile menu by pressing **Alt-F**, then select **U**ndelete.

PC Shell runs Undelete and displays a list of the deleted files in the selected directory.

To see deleted files in other directories

Start Undelete, then press **Tab** to select the Tree List window. Use the **up arrow** and **down arrow** to select the directory.

The list of deleted files changes to display the deleted files in the directory you select.

To find deleted files in any directory

1. Start Undelete, then select the **F**ile menu, then select **F**ind Deleted Files.

   or

   Press **F7**.

2. Type the file name and extension. You can include the DOS wildcard characters ***** and **?**. Press **Enter**.

3. Select **O**K to continue.

Command Reference

To search for text contained in deleted files

1. Select the **F**ile menu, then select **F**ind Deleted Files.

   or

   Press **F7**.

2. Press **Tab** to select the Containing box. Type the text you want to find. Press **Enter**.

3. Select **O**K to continue.

To sort deleted files

1. Select the **O**ptions menu, then select **S**ort By.

   or

   Press **F9**.

2. Select one of the following sort options:

Name	Sorts by the file name.
Extension	Sorts by the file extension.
Size	Sorts by the size of the file in bytes.
Deleted Date And Time	Sorts by the date and time you deleted the file.
Modified Date And Time	Sorts by the date and time you last modified the file.
Di**R**ectory	Sorts by directory.
Condi**T**ion	Sorts by the condition of the file (an estimate of the chance of successful recovery).

3. To sort, select **O**K.

To select deleted files by name

1. Select the **O**ptions menu, then select Select **B**y Name.

   or

   Press **F5**.

2. Type the file name and extension. You can include the DOS wildcard characters * and ?. Press Enter.

3. Select OK.

To view a deleted file

1. Select the deleted file(s) you want to view.

2. Select the File menu, then select View File.

   or

   Press F4

3. Press Tab to select the File Viewer window. Use the cursor keys to move around in the window.

4. After viewing the file, press Tab to select any other window, then press F4.

To undelete a file to another drive or directory (recommended)

1. Select the file(s) you want to undelete.

2. Select the File menu, then select Undelete To.

3. Select the drive. Select OK.

4. Type the path and press Enter. Select OK.

   If possible, the file is undeleted automatically.

To undelete a file to the same directory

1. Select the file(s) you want to undelete.

2. Select the File menu, then select Undelete.

   or

   Press F8.

3. Type a new first letter for the file name. Select OK by pressing Alt-O.

   If possible, the file is undeleted automatically.

To undelete a file manually

1. Select the File menu, then select Advanced Undelete, then select Manual Undelete.

2. Type a new first letter for the file name. Select **O**K by pressing **Alt-O**.
3. Select from the following commands:

   Add Cluster   Adds the currently selected cluster to the "file-to-be."

   Skip Cluster   Skips the current cluster and goes to the next cluster.

   View File   Displays what you have added to the "file-to-be" so far.

   Move   Change the position of a cluster in the "file-to-be."

   Delete   Deletes the cluster from the "file-to-be."

   Update   Collects the added clusters and saves them as a file. Type a file name and extension, then select **O**K.

Cautions

Do not run Undelete from within Windows.

If you accidentally delete a file, do not use the disk again until you run Undelete; otherwise, you may lose or destroy your data (because DOS may overwrite the deleted file with another file).

Notes

If you need to undelete a file on a floppy disk, copy the disk and use the copied disk to recover your deleted file. After you recover the file, you can copy the file back to the original disk. You must use Disk Copy (not File Copy) to copy the first disk to the second disk.

Undelete first checks for Delete Sentry protection and uses that method to undelete files. If the deleted files do not have Delete Sentry protection, Undelete next checks for Delete Tracker protection and uses that method to undelete files. If the deleted files do not have Delete Tracker protection, Undelete uses the standard DOS method.

Unformat

Beg / Int / Adv *Unformat*

Purpose

Recovers disk files accidentally deleted by using the DOS FORMAT command. Rebuilds the File Allocation Table and root directory from information in the Mirror file (if available).

To run Unformat

1. Type **UNFORMAT** at the DOS prompt and press **Enter**.

2. Select the disk you want to unformat. Select **O**K.

3. If you used Mirror on this disk, select **Y**es. If not, select **N**o. (If you don't know, select **Y**es.)

   Unformat begins to analyze the disk. The Unformat box displays a map of the disk and the status of the unformatting. A message appears if Unformat cannot unformat the disk. Select **CO**ntinue.

   If Unformat cannot unformat the disk, it still may be possible to undelete some of the lost files. See *Undelete* for details.

4. If Unformat can unformat the disk, it asks whether you want to continue. To continue, select **O**K.

5. When unformatting is complete, select **O**K.

Caution

Do not use Unformat as an experiment to see whether the program works. If you run Unformat unnecessarily, you could lose your files.

Notes

Because Unformat uses information about your disk that is created by the Mirror function, run Mirror periodically to ensure that the information exists. See *Mirror* for details.

If you are using an AT&T, Burroughs, or COMPAQ computer, Unformat cannot recover lost data if you used FORMAT.COM. On these computers, FORMAT.COM

Command Reference

erases the disk (nothing is left to recover). A good technique is to delete FORMAT.COM from your hard disk and use PCFORMAT.COM (which is included with PC Tools) instead.

Utilities

Beg / Int / Adv **DESKTOP**

Purpose

Provides hotkey selection, an ASCII table, and a program to unload PC Tools Desktop from your computer's memory.

To access Utilities

From the main **D**esktop menu, select **U**tilities.

To change hotkey selections

1. From the **U**tilities menu, select **H**otkey Selection.

2. You can change the following hotkeys:

   Desktop Hotkey
   Clipboard Paste
   Clipboard Copy
   Screen Autodial

   Select the hotkey you want to change by using the **up arrow** or **down arrow**.

3. Press the key combination you want to use for the hotkey. Select a combination which does not interfere with other hotkeys you may use.

To use the ASCII table

1. From the **U**tilities menu, select **A**SCII Table.

2. Press the character you want to find.

   or

   Use the cursor keys to scroll through the table.

To unload PC Tools Desktop

1. From the **U**tilities menu, select **U**nload PC Tools Desktop.

2. Select **U**nload.

Verify Disk

Int / Adv *PCSHELL*

Purpose

Confirms that DOS can read all the data on your disk. Checks data in files and directories and also checks unused space on the disk.

To verify a disk

1. Select the disk you want to verify. Press **Ctrl-A**, **Ctrl-B**, or **Ctrl-C** to select drive A, B, or C, respectively.

   or

   Click the drive letter on the drive line of the main PC Shell screen.

2. Select the **D**isk menu by pressing **Alt-D**, then select **V**erify.

3. To verify the selected disk, select **V**erify. If Verify finds a bad sector, select **V**erify again to continue verifying the disk or select **C**ancel to stop verifying the disk.

   PC Shell flags any bad sector not previously marked and displays the sector number and the location of the bad sector. PC Shell reports the sector's location as part of the DOS system area, part of an existing file, or as space available for use.

   If the bad sector was available for use, PC Shell marks that sector as a bad sector so that DOS does not use the bad sector to store one of your files. If a bad sector is in use by a file or subdirectory, PC Shell displays a message advising you to run the Compress

Surface Scan option in order to move the data to a safe area elsewhere on the disk.

4. Select Cancel to return to the main PC Shell screen.

Verify File

Int / Adv   *PCSHELL*

Purpose

Reads all the sectors in a file to make sure that DOS can read the entire file without errors.

To verify a file

1. Select the file(s) you want to verify.

2. Select the File menu by pressing Alt-F, then select VerifY File.

   The current file name and extension appear in the File Verify dialog box. As Verify reads the file, the sector number changes.

   If Verify discovers no errors, a message stating that the file is OK appears in the File Verify dialog box. If you selected more than one file, Verify continues through the list of selected files.

   If Verify discovers an error, it displays the location of the logical sector containing the error in the File Verify dialog box.

3. To repair a sector, select View/Edit from the File Verify dialog box.

   Select Save (by pressing F5) to rewrite the sector information, without the error, back onto your disk.

4. Select Cancel to return to the main PC Shell screen. This procedure recovers as much of your data as possible.

View/Edit Disk

Adv   *PCSHELL*

Purpose

Enables you to view, edit, or change any sector on the disk, whether or not the sector is part of a DOS file.

To view a disk

1. Select the disk you want to view. Press **Ctrl-A**, **Ctrl-B**, or **Ctrl-C** to select drive A, B, or C, respectively.

   or

   Click the drive letter on the drive line of the main PC Shell screen.

2. Select the **D**isk menu by pressing **Alt-D**, then select View/**E**dit.

   The following function keys are available in View mode:

Key	Description
F6	Enables you to select the sector to view. Select one of the sector options.
F7	Switches to Edit mode.
F8	Displays the name of the file that occupies the sector.
Home	Moves to the first sector on the disk.
End	Moves to the last sector on the disk.
PgUp	Repositions the display to the preceding half-sector.
PgDn	Repositions the display to the next half-sector.

3. If you press **F6**, select one of the following sector options.

   Boot Sector   First **F**AT Sector   Moves to the first byte of the disk boot record.

   First **F**AT Sector   Moves to the first byte of the File Allocation Table.

   First **R**oot Sector   Moves to the first byte of the root directory.

   First **D**ata Sector   Moves to the first byte of the first data sector.

   Change C**L**uster   Moves to the cluster whose number you specify.

   Change **S**ector   Moves to the sector whose number you specify.

   After making a selection from the dialog box, select **O**K to complete the Change Sector process.

4. Press **Esc** or **F3** to return to the main PC Shell screen.

To edit a sector of a disk

1. Select the disk you want to edit. Press **Ctrl-A**, **Ctrl-B**, or **Ctrl-C** to select drive A, B, or C, respectively.

   or

   Click the drive letter on the drive line of the main PC Shell screen.

2. Select the **D**isk menu by pressing **Alt-D**, then select View/**E**dit.

3. Press **F7** and select Edit from the Disk View/Edit dialog box.

   The following function keys are available in Edit mode:

F8	Switches between Hex values and ASCII text.
F5	Saves changes and returns to View mode.
Home	Moves to the first byte in the sector.
End	Moves to the last byte in the sector.
PgUp	Repositions the display to the preceding half-sector.
PgDn	Repositions the display to the next half-sector.
Esc or **F3**	Exits to the main PC Shell.

4. Use the arrow keys to move the cursor to the first byte you want to edit.

5. Type the new value.

6. To save the changes, press **F5**.

Caution

Before making changes to any sector of the disk with this command, you need a working knowledge of ASCII and hexadecimal values and of sector bytes. Making improper changes to your files with the View/Edit command can make your programs or your computer inoperable.

View File Contents

Beg / Int / Adv   *PCSHELL, VIEW*

Purpose

Displays a file in its regular format so that you can see the contents of the file.

To view a file's contents

1. Select the file(s) you want to view.

   Available viewers include popular word processors, spreadsheets, and databases.

2. Select the **F**ile menu, then select **V**iew File Contents.

   or

   Press **F2**.

Virus Defend

Beg / Int / Adv   **VDEFEND**

Purpose

VDefend is a memory-resident program that defends your system from over 400 viruses.

To run VDefend

Type **VDEFEND** at the DOS prompt, then press **Enter**.

To run VDefend when you boot your computer

Add the following line to your AUTOEXEC.BAT file:

VDEFEND

Notes

Run VDefend every time you reboot your computer.

If VDefend finds a virus, it displays a message that includes the name of the program. Press any key to continue. You should delete that program file and replace it with an uninfected copy from the original disk(s).

If VDefend detects low-level formatting, it displays a message. Select one of the following options:

C**O**ntinue	Enables the formatting to continue. Select this option if you initiated the formatting.

Stop	Stops the formatting. Select this option if you did not initiate the formatting.
Boot	Reboots your computer. Select this option if you tried **S**top and the message appeared again.

Wipe

Beg / Int / Adv **WIPE**

Purpose

Deletes files by erasing them from the disk and overwriting the disk areas ensuring that no one can extract sensitive data from the disks. Wipe can delete files, directories, or entire disks.

To start Wipe

Type **WIPE** at the DOS prompt, then press **Enter**.

To wipe files

1. Select **F**ile from the Wipe main menu.

2. To change drives, select **D**rive by pressing **Alt-D**. Select the drive, then select **O**K.

3. To change directories, select D**I**rectory by pressing **Alt-I**. Select the directory, then select **O**K by pressing **Alt-O**.

4. Type the name of the file(s) you want to delete. You can include the DOS wildcard characters **?** and *****.

5. Select from the following options :

   Con**F**irm Each File (**Alt-F**) displays the name of each file before wiping it and enables you to select whether to wipe or skip the file.

   Include **S**ubdirectories (**Alt-S**) wipes matching files in subdirectories of the selected directory.

Include **H**idden Files (**Alt-H**) wipes matching files which are hidden.

Include **R**ead-Only Files (**Alt-R**) wipes matching files which are read-only.

6. Select the type of files to wipe:

    Only **M**odified Files (by pressing **Alt-M**) wipes only those files whose archive bit is set.

    Only U**N**modified Files (by pressing **Alt-N**) wipes only those files whose archive bit is not set.

    Modified **A**nd Unmodified Files (by pressing **Alt-A**) wipes files regardless of their archive bit.

7. Select the type of wipe you want to use:

    Wipe Files (**Alt-W**) deletes selected files, then overwrites their disk areas.

    Clear Only **U**nused File Space (**Alt-U**) wipes only the unused disk space of the selected files (and does not affect the files).

    D**E**lete Files (**Alt-E**) deletes the files, but does not wipe them.

8. Select the age of files to wipe:

    O**L**der Than (**Alt-L**) wipes only those files whose date/time is earlier than or the same as the date/time you enter.

    E**Q**ual To (**Alt-Q**) wipes only those files whose date/time is the same as the date/time you enter.

    Younger Than (**Alt-Y**) wipes only those files whose date/time is later than or the same as the date/time you enter.

    Any Date/**T**ime (**Alt-T**) wipes files regardless of their date/time.

9. To start the wipe, select **O**K by pressing **Alt-O**.

    If you selected Con**F**irm Each File, Wipe displays each file name. Select **W**ipe to wipe the file or **S**kip to go to the next file without wiping the current file.

To wipe a disk

1. Select **D**isk from the Wipe main menu.

2. To change drives, select Change **D**rive, then select the drive you want to wipe, then select **O**K.

3. Select the parts of the disk you want to wipe:

   Wipe Disk wipes the entire disk.

   Clear Only **U**nused Space wipes only that space containing previously deleted data.

4. Select **O**K.

5. To confirm the wipe, select **W**ipe. To cancel the wipe, select **S**top, then **C**ancel.

To configure wipe options

1. Select **C**onfigure from the Wipe main menu.

2. Select the wipe method you want to use:

   Fast Wipe overwrites the area with a character you select.

   DOD Wipe satisfies the U.S. Department of Defense standards for wiping data from disks.

3. Select the overwrite character (in decimal ASCII) and the number of times to repeat the overwrite.

4. To save this configuration, select **S**ave Config.

5. Select **O**K.

Caution

You cannot undelete files, directories, or drives deleted by Wipe. Use Wipe only if you are sure you will never want to undelete the deleted files.

Write Protection

Beg / Int / Adv　　　　　　　　　　　　*DATAMON*

Purpose

Prevents data, program, or system files from being deleted, replaced, or damaged by accident or by deliberate action. Alerts you to viruses which may attempt to alter your protected files.

To run Write Protection

1. From the Data Monitor main menu, select Write Protection.

2. Select Load Write Protection by pressing Alt-L.

3. To protect the entire disk, select Entire Disk by pressing Alt-E.

4. To protect system areas, including the boot sector and File Allocation Table, select System Areas by pressing Alt-S.

5. To protect all floppy drives, select Protect Floppy Drives by pressing Alt-P.

6. To protect files that you specify, select File Types Listed Below by pressing Alt-F. In the Include and Exclude boxes, type the file specifications. You can include the DOS wildcard characters ? and *.

7. Select OK by pressing Alt-O.

To work with write-protected files

When you are about to delete, replace, or change a write-protected file, a dialog box appears.

To cancel the operation, select Cancel. To enable the operation, select COntinue. To turn off Write Protection, select Disable.

Note

To use Write Protection on a network, run Data Monitor after the network drivers.

Zoom the Current Window

Beg / Int / Adv **PCSHELL**

Purpose

Toggles the active window between a small window and a full-screen display.

To zoom or unzoom the current window

1. Use **Tab** to select the window you want to zoom or unzoom.

2. Press **Alt-space** bar, then select MAximize to zoom or **R**estore to unzoom.

    or

    Press **F8**.

Index

A

appointments, 7-12
ASCII
    searching for text strings, 113-115
    tables, 135
    text files, 71-73
autosave, 11-12

B

backup copies, 31-34

C

caching data, 98
calculators, 13-14
calendars, 7-10
clusters (mapping), 56-57, 67-68
commands
    canceling, 4
    DOS maintenance, 104-105
    help in locating and describing, 70
    keyboard, 3-4
    recalling past, 108
    selecting, 5
configuring colors, 99
copying
    files, 29-31, 45-46
    floppy disks, 28-29
    text, 15-16

D

databases
    creating, 35-37
    field names, 39
    forms, 39-40
    guidelines, 34-35
    printing, 40
    records, 37-39
    sorting, 39

date/time
    setting, 117
    stamp, 12, 41
dBASE files (repairing), 66-67
deleting
    appointments, 8, 9
    database records, 37-38
    directories, 49-50
    disks, 144
    fax entries, 61
    files, 14-15, 42, 142-144
    PC Shell from memory, 109
Desktop (unloading), 135-136
desktop organizers, 46
dialing phone numbers, 13, 40-41
Direct Memory Access (DMA), 34
directories
    creating, 48
    deleting, 49-50
    hiding copies of root, 80-81
    modifying attributes, 50-51
    moving files, 85-86
    moving subdirectories, 50
    phone, 125-127
    printing file lists, 107
    protecting, 47
    rebuilding root, 134-135
    recovering, 130-133
    renaming, 48-49
    searching for, 121-122
    sorting, 26
    sorting files, 120-121
disk drives
    changing, 14
    displaying information, 123
disks
    comparing, 23-24
    copying, 28-29
    deleting, 144
    formatting, 68-70, 100-101
    indicating access, 55-56
    mapping, 56-57
    obtaining information, 55

renaming volume labels, 110
repairing, 51-54
searching for strings, 113-114
transferring DOS system files to, 78-79
unformatting, 134-135
verifying, 136
viewing and editing, 138-139
DOS
displaying system information, 122-123
maintenance commands, 104-105
recalling past commands, 108
transferring system files to disk, 78-79

E

editing
appointments, 9
database records, 37
disks, 138-139
fax destination entries, 61
field names, 39
files, 71-72
text, 16
text files, 57-58
electronic mail, 89, 128-130
exiting PC Shell, 58

F

FAT (file allocation table)
hiding copies of, 80-81
rebuilding, 134-135
faxes, 58-61
field names, 39
files
backups, 32
changing attributes, 12
changing display options, 65
comparing, 24-25
compressing, 25-28
copying, 29-31, 45-46
deleting, 14-15, 42, 142-144
displaying, 81-83
displaying information, 118
editing, 57-58, 71-72
finding duplicates, 63-64
fragmentation, 26
loading, 11
mapping, 67-68
moving, 85-86
preventing accidental deletion, 43-44
printing, 105-106
printing lists of, 107
protecting, 47, 101-103, 145
recovering, 130-135
renaming, 109-110
repairing, 66-67, 72-73
retrieved, 64-65
saving, 11
searching for, 61-63, 76-78
searching for strings, 114-115
selecting and sorting, 3-6, 64-65
sending as electronic mail, 89
sending by remote control, 18-20
sorting in directories, 120-121
transferring DOS system to disk, 78-79
unselecting, 6
verifying, 137
viewing, 71-72, 107, 140-141
formatting
data disks, 68-70
disks, 100-101
low-level, 53
fragmentation, 26
function keys (defining), 117-118

H

hard drives
backups, 31-34
parking heads, 97
help, 70
hexadecimal values, 71-73
hexidecimals, 113-115
hiding
copies of FAT and root directory, 80-81

Index

database records, 38
lists, 73
hotkeys, 135

K

keyboard
    commands, 3-4
    configuring, 100
    displaying information, 123
keyboard shortcuts, PC Shell, 4

L

linking laptop and desktop PCs, 44-46
lists
    displaying, 81-83
    hiding, 73
    to-do, 10
loading
    database forms, 40
    files, 11
Lotus 1-2-3 files (repairing), 66

M

macros, 73-76
mapping memory, 79-80
memory
    caching data, 98
    deleting PC Shell from, 109
    displaying information, 123
    freeing before running programs, 107
    information, 79
    mapping, 79-80
menus (selecting), 4-5
modems, 123-129
mouse, 5-6
    configuring, 100
    displaying information, 123
moving
    files, 85-86
    windows, 119-120

N

networks
    displaying information, 122-123
    information, 86-87
    using PC Tools, 6-7

O

outlines, 96-97

P

parking read/write heads, 97
pasting text, 16
PC Shell, 104-105
    deleting from memory, 109
    exiting, 58
    saving configurations, 112
PC Tools
    applications, 1-2
    configuring, 98-100
    keyboard commands, 3-4
    mouse, 5-6
    on networks, 6-7
PCs
    linking laptop and desktop, 44-46
    running by remote control, 16-23
phone directories, 125-127
phone numbers, 13, 40-41
printing
    databases, 40
    file lists, 107
    files, 105-106
    schedules, 11
Program List (changing), 84-85
programs
    freeing memory before running, 107
    running, 111
protecting
    files, 47, 101-103, 145
    from accidental file deletion, 43-44

R

records, 37-39
remote control (running)PCs, 16-23
renaming
    disk volume labels, 110
    files, 109-110
restoring database records, 38
root directory
    hiding copies of, 80-81

rebuilding, 134-135
running
    PCs by remote control, 16-23
    programs, 111

S

saving
    files, 11
    outlines, 97
    PC Shell configurations, 112
schedules, 9-11
screens
    clearing, 112-113
    configuring, 116-118
scrolling windows, 6
searching for
    directories, 121-122
    files, 61-64, 76-78
    strings, 113-114
    text, 39
sectors
    editing, 71-72
    mapping, 56-57
    repairing, 72-73
    viewing and editing, 138-139

sorting files in directories, 120-121
strings, 113-114
Symphony files (repairing), 66-67

T

text
    copying and pasting, 15-16
    editing, 16
    files, 57-58
    outlines, 96-97
    searching for, 39
to-do lists, 10

V

viruses, 33
    defending, 141-142

W-Z

windows
    scrolling, 6
    sizing or moving, 119-120
word processing, 88-95
zooming, 146